DICKENS'S
ENGLAND

DICKENS'S ENGLAND

by

Michael & Mollie Hardwick

Photography by

Michael Hardwick

J. M. DENT & SONS LTD

LONDON

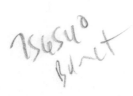

Contents

List of Illustrations

Preface

This book does not set out to be an index to all the buildings, scenes and localities mentioned in the writings of Charles Dickens and associated with his life: many have vanished, or are changed beyond recognition, and his own descriptions are their best memorial. What it does attempt is to tell the story of Dickens's life against the scenes he knew, his homes, schools, lodgings, and the towns and villages he visited, and to show how his keen observation and brilliant descriptive powers transmuted them into the backgrounds of his novels and stories.

There have been many works of topographical Dickensiana in the past, but all, to the best of our knowledge, have dwelt only on what was, rather than on what remains. This book conducts the reader to every English scene and building connected by any significance with Dickens which is still to be seen today, a century after his death. Thanks to the English passion for demolition, many places he knew personally and immortalized in his books have disappeared: the charming house in Devonshire Terrace, Marylebone, for example, where he lived at the most productive period in his life, was wantonly destroyed only a few years ago. Much of what is affectionately known as 'Dickens's London', the London of Fagin, Dombey and Little Dorrit, has fallen to bombs even where the demolishers' hammers had spared it.

But much, fortunately, is left: far more than can be found in connection with any other nineteenth-century English author.

Such was Dickens's personal magic, and such the enormous fame he enjoyed in his lifetime (increased, not diminished, by his death), that any house he lived in, visited or wrote about was remembered for his sake. To study the man and his impact on those who knew him is to understand this completely. In Kent, his chosen county and cradle of his genius, the pride in him is strongest, the houses and scenes most abounding; but it is possible to follow him to many other parts of the country and to find something of him in unassuming houses and quaint corners, lonely churches and stately homes, places that knew him and can help to bring him to life for us. Many are well worth a visit for their own sake.

By happy chance it has been possible to photograph Dickens's England for this book without much impingement of twentieth-century anachronisms and eyesores. Some of the scenes have never been depicted before.

Michael and Mollie Hardwick

Acknowledgments

Our thanks are due to the following people: Sir Felix Aylmer; Lord Cobbold, Knebworth House; Mr W. G. Coe, manager of Ye Olde King's Head, Chigwell; Mr M. D. Dolamore, manager of the Great White Horse, Ipswich; Mrs Eade, Bleak House, Broadstairs; The Reverend E. J. Gargery, chairman, Deal branch of the Dickens Fellowship; Mr M. Hallabrin, 11 Ordnance Terrace, Chatham; Miss Hewlett, headmistress of Gadshill Place School; Miss Ann Hoffmann, Authors' Research Services, Rotherfield, Sussex; Mr A. J. Howarth, Curator of Art, Portsmouth City Museums; Mr M. V. Mackie, Restoration House, Rochester; Mr R. J. Marsh, Borough Librarian of Rochester; Mr and Mrs Miles, of the Leather Bottle, Cobham; Mr Noyes, manager of Rules Restaurant; Miss M. Pillers, Dickens House, 48 Doughty Street; Mr Prechezer, manager of the Royal Victoria and Bull, Rochester; Dr Michael Slater, Editor of *The Dickensian*; Mr Leslie Staples, former Editor of *The Dickensian;* Truman, Hanbury, Buxton & Co. Ltd; Mr P. D. R. Venning, Wylde's Farm, Hampstead.

1

The Man and the Places

'Excepting always the haunts and associations of his childhood,' said Dickens's friend and biographer, John Forster, 'Dickens had no particular sentiment of locality, and any special regard for houses he had lived in was not a thing noticeable in him.'

It is the first paradox in the paradoxical life of the author who, more than any, is associated with geographical localities and individual buildings. The last significant words he wrote were a description of place: the effect of summer sunlight and morning air on ancient Rochester Cathedral, subduing its earthy odour and preaching the Resurrection and the Life. Yet this is less factual description than allegory: his own deeply intuitive sense of the supernormal ('almost Spiritualistic', comments Forster disapprovingly) showed him the image of his own tired, sick, fifty-eight-year-old body equated with Rochester Cathedral, the building so closely identified with his boyhood, to which death would bring a new life on that June morning in 1870.

Perhaps he was uninvolved with place because he was, in a sense, part of it. To study Dickens in depth is to conclude that he had a vitality surpassing that of ordinary mortals, making him almost a force of nature in himself. His effect on his contemporaries was that of a charge of electricity. His face had enough life in it for fifty human beings, said one. To Jane Carlyle he was 'like steel', sharp and white-hot. When he entered a room, said someone else, it was as though the sun came out. He was perfectly

1

aware of this incandescent quality in himself ('galwanic' would have been his Wellerian word for it) and facetiously gave himself such nicknames as The Sparkler and The Gas Light Boy. For all his human (though not earthy) attributes, there was in him much of the elemental, that wandering spirit so baffling to ghost-hunters. He was Mercury; he was Ariel, who might be imprisoned in a tree but could never submit to domestication. All accounts of him emphasize his passion for immensely long walks, for the open air (in his later years he acquired a permanent sailor-like tan), his restlessness, which caused him to move house more frequently than most Victorians and to transport his family, servants and effects all over the Continent at the drop of a hat, with no particular benefit to them but much to him. Such persons do not belong to houses, or to places at all. He was in essence a cosmic being, rather than a terrestrial one. Among his esoteric interests was astrology. He said little of it, for it was hardly a respectable subject in his time, but glimpses of it peep out of his writings. In *Barnaby Rudge*, an early novel, he reflects that: 'The thoughts of worldly men are for ever regulated by a moral law of gravitation which, like the physical one, holds them down to earth . . . there are no signs in the sun, or in the moon, or in the stars, for their reading. They are like some wise men who, learning to know each planet by its Latin name, have quite forgotten such small heavenly constellations as Charity . . . and who, looking upward to the spangled sky, see nothing there but the reflection of their own great wisdom and book-learning.'

Captain Cuttle of *Dombey and Son*, who is in part the sailor figure on whom it amused Dickens, in youth and age, to model his appearance, muses thus on an imaginary nautical instrument for weighing stars: 'Look'ee here! *here's* a collection of 'em. Earth, air, or water. Ah! it's a fine thing to understand 'em. And yet it's a fine thing *not* to understand 'em. I hardly know which is best. It's so comfortable to sit here and feel that you might be weighed, measured, magnified, electrified, polarized—played the very devil with; and never know how.'

Dickens was born under the sign of Aquarius which, by a freak of astrology, is an airy and not a watery sign. Yet the element of water which flows through Dickens's life is present too. The present authors experimented some time ago by giving the time and place of Dickens's birth to an astrologer who was not told the name of the subject, and in any case had no knowledge of Dickens's character or history. Her conclusions, presented in the form of a horoscope, were amazingly accurate, a near-perfect diagnosis of Dickens. She begins by saying: 'The symbol for Aquarius is an angel pouring out living water for all mankind, and this is exemplified in the subject, who makes no difference between persons when working for a cause. . . . Neptune in his chart has obviously had a great effect on his powers of imagination.'

In fact, water was an unconscious symbol to him of many things: of life itself, of movement, and rivers and seas in his books are more personally and vividly felt and described than are places. At Brighton he is amused to 'see the little gilt toys going up and down before the mighty sea, and thinking nothing of it'. At Broadstairs, as he sits in his eyrie on the cliff, Fort House, the sea blows great guns for him, or winks like a drowsy lion; and here he sat on the shore, and read Tennyson, and told Forster in a remarkable passage how the poetry 'dried up the waters' for him, and 'showed me all the mermen and mermaids, at the bottom of the ocean, together with millions of queer creatures, half-fish and half-fungus, looking down into all manner of coral caves and seaweed conservatories'. He transports the sea of Broadstairs to Yarmouth in *David Copperfield*, and makes it serve as an instrument of retribution by drowning Steerforth, seducer of innocence.

Sea-dwellings are symbols of bliss to him. The childish love of David and Little Em'ly begins among the shells and pebbles of Yarmouth Beach, and David's zenith of enchantment is the little ship's cabin of a bedroom in the stern of Dan'l Peggotty's upturned boat. Just as, in *The Mystery of Edwin Drood*, the last book of all, Rosa Bud's first blush of love comes to her in that room 'like a dream': the neat shining admiral's cabin of an apartment lent to her by the attractive ex-sailor Mr Tartar, where he pays to her all the homage due to the First Lady of the Admiralty—or, more aptly, the First Fairy of the Sea.

Rivers, too, were principal actors in his works. The Thames, by which was his first adult London lodging, at 15 Buckingham Street, is sometimes a monster, filth-filled by the city's inadequate sewerage system (though, with the reticence of his times, he left out the more squalid details, just as in *Our Mutual Friend* he forbore to point out that Boffin's Golden Dust-Heap consisted largely of ordure). The Thames dominates *Our Mutual Friend*

3

even more aggressively than the dust-heap. It bears along the floating corpse thought to be John Harmon, it provides Rogue Riderhood with his dreadful trade, it carries along the story of old Betty Higden (a young river here, dimpling, unspoilt), it attends on the marriage-feast at Greenwich of Bella and John, whose fare is symbolically a multitude of glittering, rainbow-hued fish. It brings Lizzie to the dramatic rescue of Wrayburn.

In *Great Expectations* it shares the cast-list with the human actors, a conspirator with Pip and Herbert Pocket to get the convict Magwitch out of the country. In *Oliver Twist*, flowing darkly by London Bridge, it hears Nancy telling the tale that will lead to her murder. It bears Rosa and Tartar on an idyllic voyage to happiness in *Edwin Drood*; it receives the bloodstained clothes in which Jonas Chuzzlewit murdered Tigg Montague. In *The Old Curiosity Shop* it is the sinister background for Quilp the dwarf, in his hideout on the Surrey side of the river, 'Quilp's Wharf . . . a small, rat-infested, dreary yard'.

Dickens could analyse himself brilliantly, when emotional conflicts were not involved, and did so when he said, 'Running water is favourable to day-dreams, and a strong tidal river is the best of running water for mine'. With landscape, however, he is less happy. The countryside of the novels is rather the townsman's picture-postcard world than the actual scene of Georgian hovels without amenities, of sheep, cattle and pigs driven brutally on tired feet to their deaths at Smithfield, of the peasants who, when the lunatic calling himself Sir William Courtenay rode up to their doors in 1838 and announced himself to be Jesus Christ, believed and followed him. The country is simply the converse of the town —'better than chimney-pots,' says Weller to Pickwick—unless it is designed to serve some symbolical purpose as it does throughout the journeyings of Nell and her grandfather, or during the murder of Tigg. Dingley Dell, the Nicklebys' retreat at rural Bow, the Maylies' Chertsey home where Oliver finds happiness, all are straightforward roses-round-the-door regions with the nastiness left out.

For he did omit much from his descriptions. Like Mrs General in *Little Dorrit*, the public 'was not to be told of anything shocking'; shocking, that is, to its sense of propriety, though its sensibilities might be endlessly harrowed. A time without sanitation, as we know it, without anaesthetics, without special legislation

4

for children, without compassion for animals, without any concept of personal hygiene or of the necessity for sex education, would have been impossible for Dickens, eager reformer as he was, to set down on paper without incurring universal execration and putting himself out of business. Therefore it is that we may applaud his striking pictures of such slums as Tom All-Alone's in *Bleak House* and, in the same book, of the horrible overflowing town burial-ground where Nemo lies, but for the reality of such places must look to such factual records as Henry Mayhew's *London Labour and the London Poor*.*

Dickens is credited with a passion for London; he entertained no such thing. His education for living was in her streets, he was a natural Cockney, though not a native; he greedily observed and absorbed her, knew her with Weller's 'extensive and peculiar' knowledge; but he did not, in any romantic sense, love her. He was not, indeed, romantic at all. A similar infatuation for old buildings has been attributed to him; in fact he disliked them. Ancient inns, like the Maypole at Chigwell in *Barnaby Rudge* and that cosy house on Marlborough Downs where Tom Smart, the Bagman of *The Pickwick Papers*, had his curious adventure with the old chair, amuse Dickens. They are 'quaint', blackened with age, leaning over sideways, interestingly populated by ghosts, the repositories for fine food and liquor, sometimes serving as contrasting backgrounds for fresh youth. But if he, the progressive modern man with the improvement of society at heart, had had his way, every such building would have been demolished and replaced by the Victorian equivalent of the concrete block: functional, aseptic, no-nonsense affairs where neither ghost, mouse, not sinister wayfarer dare set foot.

The house of Mrs Clennam in *Little Dorrit* is described as: 'so dingy as to be all but black . . . it had been propped up . . . and was leaning on some half-dozen gigantic crutches: which gymnasium for the neighbouring cats, weather-stained, smoke-blackened, and overgrown with weeds, appeared in these latter days to be no very sure reliance.' Arthur Clennam comments: 'Nothing changed. Dark and miserable as ever.' The front door 'had a projecting canopy in carved work, of festooned jack-towels and children's heads with water on the brain'. By twentieth-century standards

* published 1851–62. Mayhew also wrote *The Criminal Prisons of London* (in collaboration with John Binny, 1862) and *London Characters* (1874).

5

of taste the house was a highly desirable residence, of William and Mary or Queen Anne date: the porch canopy either imitated or was the work of Grinling Gibbons. To Dickens it was tasteless, ridiculous, only fit to be used as a symbol of corruption. He belonged to a generation which despised the architecture of the previous two centuries and which, while tolerating until mid-century or thereabouts increasingly inferior echoes of it, then erupted jubilantly into neo-Gothic and the hideous over-ornamentation and architectural vulgarity which were the direct antithesis of the rejected 'plainness' of Adam and Nash.

Yet, disliking the antique, Dickens's marvellous reporter's eye took in every detail of it and translated it into word-pictures more vivid than any photograph. That they are not accurate pictures does not matter. Any observer can describe, with no more striking results than may be seen in a surveyor's report. Dickens was not content to describe; he created. What is familiarly and affectionately known as 'Dickens's London' is not, in fact, the London of his day at all, but a fantastic city of his own building. He could not through the medium of prose emulate Hogarth, the artist he most admired, whose London leaps out at us from his works in stone and brick, almost tangible. He had not Hogarth's loving eye for place; it merely provided for him backgrounds for his characters, for his absorbed and absorbing studies of people. Mankind was his material, the stuff of life to him, his audience, his victim and his pensioner.

Only in Kent does anything like real affection creep into his descriptions. Again and again he returns for his settings to Rochester and Chatham, and makes them peculiarly his own, as he felt them to be: 'I have many happy recollections connected with Kent and am scarcely less interested in it than if I had been a Kentish man bred and born, and had resided in the county all my life.' And yet it is difficult not to feel that it was not the county itself, its orchards and gardens, ruins and country houses, which held him by any physical charms; it was, rather, those 'recollections' of his happy Chatham childhood, before his life was darkened and complicated by the traumatic experiences of poverty, bereavement and misplaced love. In Kent lived the ghost-boy of 'The Haunted House',* that bitter piece of self-analysis, who

* one of the collected *Christmas Stories*.

is called Master B. because he is really Master Boz: 'Ah me, ah me! No other ghost has haunted the boy's room, my friends, since I have occupied it, than the ghost of my own childhood, the ghost of my own innocence, the ghost of my own airy belief. Many a time have I pursued the phantom: never with this man's stride of mine to come up with it, never with these man's hands of mine to touch it, never more to this man's heart of mine to hold it in its purity.'

When he created David Copperfield, the character through whom he wrote his unacknowledged autobiography, he sent David to Dover for rescue, to Canterbury for the education which had been so all-important to the deprived twelve-year-old drudge at Warren's Blacking Factory, and back to Canterbury for the refuge of idealized married life with Agnes. Pip of *Great Expectations*, his next boy-narrator, learnt his hard life-lessons in the surroundings of Dickens's childhood; and young Edwin Drood came to Rochester to die. Just so did the lost boy, the ghost-boy, Master B., return in the person of the grizzled, disillusioned, middle-aged author to Gadshill Place, the house which the boy had long ago seen and desired. In Kent, if anywhere, he would find respite from the demon which drove him on, the 'old unhappy loss or want of something'; in Kent he might find, at last, a home.

And so he did; in his end was his beginning.

2

His Birthplace and 'the Birthplace of His Fancy'

The house at 1 Mile End Terrace, Landport, Portsmouth (now 393 Commercial Road), where Charles John Huffham Dickens was born on 7th February 1812, was an unprepossessing little villa, respectably middle-class, in what was then a pleasant suburb, a mile or so from the bustling hub of naval Portsmouth. Today, Commercial Road is as noisy, restless and ugly as its name implies, and a car-borne visitor to the birthplace must explore back- and side-streets in order to park. To the credit of Portsmouth Town Council, the house was bought in 1903 at public auction (for £1,125), after the death of its last private occupant, a descendant of the Dickens's own landlord, and opened to the public as a Dickens museum. It was much renovated in 1969 and has been restored to its apparent original condition. A visit is well worth a few minutes' exasperation amongst the ceaseless traffic of Commercial Road.

Tradition says that Charles Dickens was born in the front bedroom, overlooking what was a much quieter highway in 1812. If it was not there, it was its back counterpart, with its then pleasant garden outlook; for there are only the two rooms up, two down, and two attics; not much for the £35 a year John Dickens had to pay for it out of his Navy Pay Clerk's salary of £110. The proportion was unfavourable, as Mr Micawber, in *David Copperfield*, for whom John Dickens was the model, would readily have agreed: 'My other piece of advice, Copperfield, you

8

know. Annual income twenty pounds, annual expenditure nine-teen nineteen six, result happiness. Annual income twenty pounds, annual expenditure twenty pounds ought and six, result misery.'

The bed in which Dickens was born has been lost to posterity; its four posts may have gone for firewood a century and more ago, or become the prey of woodworm. But the couch on which he died was lovingly preserved by his family and is, ironically, to be seen at his birthplace. Four years before his death he went to Portsmouth on one of his reading tours with his manager, George Dolby: '. . . and turning the corner of a street suddenly, found ourselves in Landport Terrace.* The name of the street catching Mr Dickens's eye, he suddenly exclaimed, "By Jove! here is the place where I was born"; and acting on his suggestion, we walked up and down the terrace for some time, speculating as to which of the houses had the right to call itself his cradle. Beyond a recollection that there was a small front garden to the house he had no idea of the place—for he was only two years old when his father was removed to London from Portsmouth. As the houses were nearly all alike, and each had a small front garden, we were not much helped in our quest by Mr Dickens's recollections, and great was the laughter at his humorous conjectures. He must have lived in one house because "it looked so like his father"; another one must have been his home because it looked like the birthplace of a man who had deserted it; a third was very like the cradle of a puny, weak youngster such as he had been; and so on, through the row . . . but as none of the houses in Landport Terrace could cry out and say . . . "That boy was born here!" the mystery remained unsolved, and we passed on.'

It is no coincidence that Charles Dickens's birth occurred at the same time as David Copperfield's: a few minutes to midnight. Copperfield is the middle-aged author's own statement of account for his childhood and youth, and he began it at the very beginning. He was the second child, and first son, of John and Elizabeth Dickens, and it may be that, what with the indispensable servant of even so small a household, the new arrival brought it home to the Dickenses that their pretty house was simply not big enough. At any rate, they moved in June to a taller one with more rooms

* Dolby got the name wrong.

9

in a similarly respectable nearby locality, Hawke Street.* No. 16 is no longer there—a casualty of the Second World War—but Portsea has a surviving memorial to Dickens in the font in which he was baptized in the parish church, St Mary's, Kingston. When the old church was demolished in the 1850s the font was retained.† With proprietory pride the parishioners wished their church to have a memorial window to Dickens, but were dismayed to find that he himself, though two decades dead, was their obstacle. His rationalistic will, which forbade the mourners at his funeral to wear 'scarf, cloak, black bow, long hat-band or other revolting absurdity', had also forbidden the making of any 'monument, memorial, or testimonial whatever'. But another new church was built, and a tablet to Dickens's memory was placed in the church by the Portsmouth branch of the Dickens Fellowship in 1962.

He was only an infant when he left Portsmouth, and did not return to it often; though he did pay an especial visit in 1838 in order to refresh his mind with local colour, for he had decided upon Portsmouth as the setting for the experiences of Nicholas Nickleby and Smike with Mr Vincent Crummles's theatrical company. He would hardly recognize the town of his birth, which suffered so terribly in the Second World War. Some special providence must have preserved the small, defenceless-looking house in Mile End Terrace, leaving it standing when so much of old Portsmouth vanished in the flames. He would no doubt view Portsmouth as did Sam Weller the fallen estate of Mr Job Trotter:

* according to the indefatigable researcher Frederick G. Kitton, in his *The Dickens Country* (1905). The equally indefatigable Robert Langton, in *The Childhood and Youth of Charles Dickens* (1st edition 1883), had said that the new lodging was 'the second house beyond the boundary of Portsea', and his authority seemed to be Captain Henry James, R.N., who confirmed in 1885 to Langton that he had seen Dickens as 'the babe in long petticoats' there. Kitton was told by the then Town Clerk of Portsmouth that Hawke Street was not beyond the boundary of Portsea, and a letter from Kitton to the Portsmouth newspapers produced a Southsea lady correspondent who informed him that an old gentleman of her aquaintance (an octogenarian) lived in his youth at No. 8 Hawke Street, and he clearly remembered that the Dickens family resided at No. 16. The previous tenant was Chatterton, the musician who became harpist to Queen Victoria.

† It is preserved in St Stephen's Church, Portsea.

'This is rayther a change for the vorse, Mr Trotter, as the gen'lm'n said ven he got two doubtful shillin's and sixpenn'orth o' pocket-pieces for a good half-crown.'

In 1816 John Dickens was transferred briefly to London, and Charles, aged four, entered the first of his many London homes, in Norfolk Street, off Fitzroy Square, St Pancras. We shall meet him there again in young manhood, but his first stay was not significant. The Dickenses were in transit for another busy naval base, Chatham, in Kent, where John Dickens was to join the Pay Office.

Charles Dickens's friend and biographer, John Forster, described Chatham as 'the birthplace of his fancy'. Undoubtedly it was. It had just about everything for an Aquarian child of lively spirits and vivid imagination: the bustle of a principal naval dock-yard and military centre, the stir of a thriving town which was a coaching terminus, the sight of soldiers drilling and fighting mock battles, bands of manacled convicts being brought to and from the prison hulks, trips with his father up to Sheerness on the Navy Pay Yacht *Chatham*. Mr Pickwick gives a succinct and rational description of the delights to be found there: 'The principal productions . . . appear to be soldiers, sailors, Jews, chalk, shrimps, officers, and dockyard men. The commodities chiefly exposed for sale in the public streets are marine stores, hardbake, apples, flat-fish and oysters. The streets present a lively and animated appearance, occasioned chiefly by the conviviality of the military. It is truly delightful to a philanthropic mind, to see these gallant men staggering along under the influence of an overflow, both of animal and ardent spirits; more especially when we remember that the following them about and jesting with them, affords a cheap and innocent amusement for the boy population. . . . The consumption of tobacco in these towns must be very great; and the smell which pervades the streets must be exceedingly delicious to those who are extremely fond of smoking. A superficial traveller might object to the dirt which is their leading characteristic; but to those who view it as an indication of traffic and commercial prosperity, it is truly gratifying.'

These were adult judgments; behind them we may sense the uninhibited and uncritical rapture of a life-hungry, intensely sensitive child whose domestic background was quiet and respectable almost to a fault. Mrs Dickens was well educated, capable

11

of giving her children the groundings of what they would learn at school, even in the realm of the classics, and well-connected, being a relative of Sir John Barrow, second secretary of the Admiralty from 1804 to 1845. John Dickens, if we may go by Mr Micawber, was an eminently gentlemanly and well-conducted person, whose only serious fault was a certain looseness of the purse. Charles was fortunate to live in a place as vividly robust as Chatham. He loved the less active Rochester, its twin-town. 'If anybody present knows to a nicety where Rochester ends and Chatham begins, it is more than I do', he observed in 1854. Rochester appears endlessly in his books, under various pseudonyms. When he calls it Great Winglebury, in *Sketches by Boz*, he says: 'It has a long straggling High Street, with a great black and white clock at a small red Town Hall, half way up—a market place—a cage—an assembly room—a church—a bridge—a chapel—a theatre—a library—an inn—a pump—and a post office.' And he told a correspondent how 'I peeped about its old corners with interest and wonder when I was a very little child'.

These two towns which he was to immortalize he knew when he was at the most impressionable time of his life, in a state of contentment that he would never achieve again; a state which flourished at No. 2 Ordnance Terrace.

The present authors were fortunate enough to be able to enter the house, by courtesy of its owner, Mr M. Hallabrin. Outwardly a pleasant, conventional Georgian terrace house, it is structurally unchanged apart from the addition of modern plumbing. A front door with a pretty fanlight opens into a narrow hall; on the left is a small room which would be the Dickenses' dining-room and family living-room. Upstairs (and how often must Charles's hands have slid up and down the slender stair-rail) is the parlour proper, first-floor front, and the bedroom of John and Elizabeth Dickens. A further staircase leads to the attic floor. Here are two bedrooms; small, like all the other rooms, but the front one, above the parlour, has two windows and a fine view over the town to the dockyard. In 1817 the prospect must have been noble indeed; one likes to think that this was Charles's bedroom, and that the less demanding Fanny occupied the back one.

(As we write, the house (now No. 11) is condemned to demolition, along with the rest of the terrace, on the grounds that it is not worth restoring. Dickensians and others are opposing this further depletion of our heritage of significant buildings. Is it really beyond the capabilities of architects and planners to incorporate such old places into their schemes—or do they prefer not to try?)

It was a happy home to the Dickenses. A visitor described them as 'a most genial, loveable family . . . with something more than a ghost of gentility hovering in their company'. Here were born a brother and sister of Charles, both of whom died early. But Charles was not lonely. His gentle, musical sister Fanny was his beloved companion, and there were plenty of playmates: the Stroughills next door, George, handsome and daring, and Lucy, peach-faced, golden-haired, Charles's childhood sweetheart. At No. 5 was Mrs Newnham, an old lady who was particularly kind to the Dickens children. All these people emerged later as literary portraits. George became David Copperfield's school friend, Steerforth, Lucy kept her own name as Golden Lucy in 'The Wreck of the Golden Mary' (*Christmas Stories*), and Mrs Newnham, somewhat unkindly, was translated into the mad Miss Havisham of *Great Expectations*. She had a house full of attractions for the children, which Dickens described, calling her The Old Lady, in *Sketches by Boz*, his earliest published work: 'The little front parlour, which is the old lady's ordinary sitting-room, is a perfect picture of quiet neatness; the carpet is covered with brown holland, the glass and picture-frames are carefully enveloped in yellow muslin; the table-covers are never taken off, except when the leaves are turpentined and bees'-waxed . . . and the little nicknacks are always arranged in precisely the same manner. The greater part of these are presents from little girls whose parents live in the same row; but some of them, such as the two old-fashioned watches (which never keep the same time, one being always a quarter of an hour too slow, and the other a quarter of an hour too fast), the little picture of the Princess Charlotte and Prince Leopold as they appeared in the Royal Box at Drury Lane Theatre, and others of the same class, have been in the old lady's possession for many years.'

It is a minutely observed and clearly remembered picture of a typical house of those days, recorded by a pair of large bright eyes and a brain more astounding than anyone guessed to lodge under Charles's brown curls.

The Dickenses' servant was Mary Weller, a name which would

one day be immortalized. More fortunate than many domestics of her day, she had a neat little living-room in the basement, between the large kitchen and the cellar, which she shared with another servant, Jane Bonney. She it was whom Charles remembered sitting by his bedside in the tall house. 'Somebody (who I wonder, and which way did *she* go, when she died?) hummed the Evening Hymn to me, and I cried on the pillow—either with the remorseful consciousness of having kicked Somebody else, or because still Somebody else had hurt my feelings in the course of the day.' His lessons were given by his mother and an aunt, and he soon learnt to read. It was his greatest pleasure, for he was too delicate for the usual rough boyish games. 'A terrible boy to read', said Mary Weller of him. His first introduction to what might be called fiction was the telling of nursery tales to him by someone who may or may not have been Mary (he calls her Mercy); such horrific stories as that of Captain Murderer, a Bluebeard whose pleasure it was to behead his wives, chop them in pieces, pepper and salt them, eat the resulting pie and pick the bones. Charles shuddered, but shuddered deliciously; there seems to have been no heavy shadow over the days at Ordnance Terrace.

His mind was further excited by visits to the theatre. Rochester had a Theatre Royal of its own, at the foot of Star Hill. Here, with his cousin James Lamert, Charles first caught the theatrical fever which was never to leave him. As a building, it was no Haymarket or Covent Garden, but a small, unpretentious affair with a disproportionately large portico; but to Charles it was a palace of enchantment. Looking back to it in his essay 'Dullborough Town' (in *The Uncommercial Traveller*), he describes the shortcomings of its productions as though he had been, as a child, aware of them; but we know too much of the man to be convinced. 'Richard the Third, in a very uncomfortable cloak, had first appeared to me there, and had made my heart leap with terror by backing up against the stage-box in which I was posted, while struggling for life against the virtuous Richmond. It was within these walls that I had learnt as from a page of English history, how that wicked King slept in war-time on a sofa much too short for him, and how fearfully his conscience troubled his boots. . . .' Here, too, he acquired 'a strong veneration for Clowns' and decided that 'to marry a Columbine would be to attain the highest pitch of all human felicity'.

14

The under-equipped stock and touring companies, with their often inexpert artists, and the crude pantomimes of the Regency, were a joyful inspiration to him. From the first came the melo-dramatic speech and behaviour of the 'straight' characters in his earlier books, from the second some spark that ignited his marvellous flame of humour, and from both a passion for acting which never left him. When he revisited the Theatre Royal in manhood it had fallen upon evil days. 'It was To Let, and hopelessly so, for its old purposes; and there had been no entertainment within its walls for a long time except a Panorama; and even that had been announced as "pleasingly instructive", and I know too well the fatal meaning and the leaden import of those terrible expressions.'

In the 1880s the Theatre Royal acquired an even more 'instructive' function; it became a Conservative Club, and remains to this day the headquarters of the local Conservative Association. The large portico still straddles the pavement, but the front of the building has been entirely refaced in over-heavy stone.

In Chatham High Street was the Mitre Inn, 'the first posting-house in the town', where Nelson was said to have stayed when on duty at Chatham, his room being known as Nelson's Cabin. It had beautiful gardens and ancient dark rooms. 'None of the old rooms was ever pulled down; no old tree was ever rooted up; nothing with which there was any association of byegone times was ever removed or changed.' It was kept by Mr Tribe, a friend of the Dickens family. The small Charles and his sister used to sing duets on the dining-room table for the benefit of the company, and Dickens, looking back, was afraid that he 'must have been a horrible little nuisance to many unoffending grown-up people who were called upon to admire him'.

'But alas! these high and palmy days had taken to themselves boots, and were already walking off.' When Charles was nine the family moved to a smaller house (now demolished), 18 St Mary's Place, otherwise known as The Brook. Prints and photographs show it as a distinct come-down from Ordnance Terrace; little more than a cottage, with a tiny front garden, next door to the Providence Chapel, whose minister was the Reverend William Giles, father of Charles's schoolmaster. In his year and a half at 'Giles's' Charles was a happy and successful scholar, popular and full of fun, though still not strong enough to take part in games or the mock battles which went on in the district known as 'Tom

All-Alone's', a name which Dickens gave to the London slum where Poor Jo lived in *Bleak House*. A more avid reader than ever, he spent hours with his father's books 'in a little room upstairs to which I had access, for it adjoined my own'.

At the side of the house an attic window looked out on to St Mary's Church and its churchyard. Charles and Fanny would stand here at night and watch the stars, as he would recall idyllically in middle age: 'There was one clear shining star that used to come out in the sky before the rest, near the church spire, above the graves. It was larger and more beautiful, they thought, than all the others, and every night they watched for it, standing hand in hand at a window. Whoever saw it first cried out "I see the star!"'

This room, this window, these books which were the foundation of his literary education, were indelibly printed on his sensitive mind, and he re-created them in *David Copperfield*: 'The picture always rises in my mind of a summer evening, the boys at play in the churchyard, and I, sitting on my bed, reading as if for life. Every barn in the neighbourhood, every stone in the church, and every foot in the churchyard, has some association of its own in my mind connected with these books, and stood for some locality made famous in them.'

They were living nearer the dockyard now; its sights, sounds and smells impressed themselves for ever upon Charles: 'It resounded with the noise of hammers beating upon iron; and the great sheds or slips under which the mighty men-of-war are built, loomed business-like when contemplated from the opposite side of the river. For all that, however, the Yard made no display, but kept itself snug under hill-sides of corn-fields, hop-gardens, and orchards; its great chimneys smoking with a quiet—almost a lazy —air, like giants smoking tobacco . . . the store of cannon on the neighbouring gun-wharf, had an innocent toy-like appearance, and the one red-coated sentry on duty over them was a mere toy figure, with a clock-work movement. As the hot sunlight sparkled on him he might have passed for the identical little man who had the little gun, and whose bullets they were made of lead, lead, lead.'

Looking out to the Chatham Basin and the Medway, he could see 'the great ships standing out to sea or coming home richly laden, the active little steam-tugs confidently puffing with them to and from the sea-horizon, the fleet of barges that seem to have plucked their brown and russet sails from the ripe trees in the landscape . . . the yachts with their tiny hulls and great white sheets of canvas, the little sailing-boats bobbing to and fro on their errands of pleasure or business'.

The great ships are gone now, those old Wooden Walls of England which young Charles watched being built. The dockyard has grown to a size he would hardly credit, though not out of recognition. The church, the Clock Tower building, the ropery, the sail loft, the Terrace, Medway House, the Pay Office where John Dickens worked, would all be familiar to the child who knew them in Regency days. Along the walks are figure-heads rescued from demolished vessels; nymphs, gods and warriors shining with new paint and gilding, staring with bright, blank eyes. The old slips where Charles saw 'certain unfinished wooden walls left seasoning on the stocks', where, some half-century before his time, *Victory* had been built, are still to be seen, though the old single dock has been seriously damaged by fire in recent years. But though the ancient crafts still flourish, the boy would not comprehend the use of those sleek submarines which now swim like elegant sharks from their birthplace in the dockyard. He might well reflect, as the man Dickens reflected as he strolled about an iron-screw transport ship, the most modern of her kind in that year of 1863: 'I would require a handsome sum of money to go aboard her, at midnight by the dockyard bell, and stay aboard alone till morning; for surely she must be haunted by a crowd of ghosts of obstinate old martinets, mournfully flapping their cherubic epaulettes over the changed times.'

Beauty has gone from Chatham Basin with the coming of mechanization. No longer would Charles see 'the pasturing sheep and kine upon the marshes . . . the crows . . . going home from the rich harvest-fields, the heron that has been out a-fishing and looks as melancholy, up there in the sky, as if it hadn't agreed with him'. The scene is ugly and flat, attractive only in that vessels are still part of its foreground, things indestructibly romantic however functional their shape.

Change had set in soon after the Dickens family left Chatham for London in 1823. The boy Charles left in a stage-coach one miserable morning, with a conviction in his heart that he was leaving childhood and happiness behind. 'Through all the years that have since passed, have I ever lost the smell of the damp straw in which I was packed—like game—and forwarded, carriage paid,

17

to the Cross Keys, Wood-street, Cheapside, London? There was no other inside passenger, and I consumed my sandwiches in solitude and dreariness, and it rained hard all the way, and I thought life sloppier than I had expected to find it.'

The man Dickens returned to Chatham by train, on a sentimental journey, and a foretaste of the complete urbanization which would overtake his beloved town was waiting for him. 'The station had swallowed up the playing-field. It was gone. The two beautiful hawthorn-trees, the hedge, the turf, and all those buttercups and daisies, had given place to the stoniest of jolting roads.' * The coach-office from which as a child he had travelled up to London in a coach romantically named Timpson's Blue-Eyed Maid had disappeared, and had been replaced by a new building housing the firm of Pickford (which still occupies it). Saddened by these and more changes, Dickens was mellowed by encounters with old friends into a more charitable mood with 'Dullborough', as he somewhat unkindly called it. 'And yet in my heart I had loved it all day, too,' he said. 'Ah! who was I that I should quarrel with the town for being changed to me, when I myself had come back, so changed, to it! All my early readings and early imaginations dated from this place, and I took them away so full of innocent construction and guileless belief, and I brought them back so worn and torn, so much the wiser and so much the worse!'

* In fact, Chatham station is hard by Ordnance Terrace, and the railway-line cuts across the view from Charles's bedroom window.

3

First Years in London

'The light mists were solemnly rising, as if to show me the world, and I had been so innocent and little there, and all beyond was so unknown and great.' The speaker is the boy Pip, in *Great Expectations*, leaving Rochester; but he speaks for his creator, leaving the happy life of Chatham for London. The change was a worse one than he had anticipated, even in the coach with its damp straw and tear-soaked sandwiches. John Dickens, for all his geniality, was a hopelessly improvident man. His spendthrift habits had brought his family first to the small house in Ordnance Terrace, and now to what Forster calls 'a small, mean tenement' in Bayham Street, Camden Town.

In fact, 16 Bayham Street, though small, was probably not as bad as all that. It has vanished now beneath the buildings of the Hampstead General and North-West London Hospital, but some of the original houses remain, cottage-sized and neat, built about 1813. Perhaps it was something of a squeeze to get the Dickens family in, now that there were six children (Frederick and Alfred had been born in 1820 and 1822). Charles's idyllic star-gazing window and book-room had gone, and in their place was a little back-garret, which he probably had to share with his small brothers. His friends had been left behind. Fanny was still very dear, but growing away from him into young womanhood; soon she would be a music student. He was very lonely, miserable and uprooted. Much of the familiar household furniture had gone the way of Charles's beloved books, to pay his father's debts. No schooling was suggested, and the bright pupil of Mr Giles's school became a drudge. 'I degenerated into cleaning his [John Dickens's] boots of a morning, and my own, and making myself useful in the work of the little house, and looking after my younger brothers and sisters. . . .'

From a distance of twenty-three years he looked back, in *Dombey and Son*, to the district he had loathed so much. Staggs's Gardens is a memory of somewhere near Bayham Street: 'a little row of houses, with little squalid patches of ground before them, fenced off with old doors, barrel staves, scraps of tarpaulin, and dead bushes; with bottomless tin kettles and exhausted iron fenders, thrust into the gaps. Here, the Staggs's Gardeners trained scarlet beans, kept fowls and rabbits, erected rotten summer-houses (one was an old boat), dried clothes, and smoked pipes'.

The railway had not yet come to devastate Camden Town in 1823, and in fact it would appear pleasantly rural to our eyes in contrast with its character today. Near Bayham Street the Fleet River still flowed above ground. Between Camden Town and Somers Town (now the hinterland of Euston) there were fields. Kentish Town was a place of cottages and market-gardens, with some fine houses still left. Chalk Farm was a real farm. The Mother Redcap public house (now on the corner of Camden Town Broadway) was a tea-garden establishment,* frequented by City folk on pleasure bent, washing down huge quantities of shrimps and winkles with ginger-beer, the gentlemen smoking pipes and cigars, the married ladies genteelly comparing confinements and admiring each other's offspring, while the unmarried ladies devoted themselves to 'chasing one another on the grass in the most playful and interesting manner, with the view of attracting the attention of . . . husbands in perspective'. † Cricket and kite-flying were indulged in where now red buses run over hidden underground railways.

---

* It served stronger refreshment, as it had done for centuries; a now vanished sign-board used to proclaim:

> *Old Mother Red Cap, according to her tale,*
> *Lived twenty and a hundred years by drinking this good ale,*
> *It was her meat, it was her drink, and medicine beside,*
> *And if she still had drunk good ale, she never would have died.*

† *Sketches by Boz.*

CHARLES DICKENS' BIRTHPLACE
FEBRUARY 7TH 1812.

DICKENS MUSEUM

*393 Commercial Road (formerly 1 Mile End Terrace), Landport, Ports-
mouth. Now a Dickens museum, it has been restored since this photograph
was taken to the condition in which the family knew it.*

2

The house of Mrs Clennam in Little Dorrit *: ' It had been propped up ...*
leaning on some half-dozen gigantic crutches.' Illustration by ' Phiz '.

3

11 (formerly 2) Ordnance Terrace, Chatham, Kent : Dickens's childhood home,
1817–21.

4

The George Inn, Borough High Street, Southwark, the only surviving galleried inn in London from Dickens's times. It is mentioned in Little Dorrit.

All that remains of the Marshalsea Prison, Borough, City of London. Dickens's father was imprisoned there.

Hungerford Stairs, Strand, London, showing Warren's Blacking Warehouse, where Dickens was employed in 1824. It was replaced by the present Embankment Gardens beside Charing Cross station.

5

6

7

22 Cleveland Street, Marylebone. Dickens lived here with his parents during his early reporting days.

25 (formerly 15) Fitzroy Street, Marylebone, where Dickens lived ▷ during his courtship of Maria Beadnell.

8

9

Furnival's Inn, Holborn, as it was when Dickens made his first married home there. Drawing by Frederick G. Kitton.

From the end of Bayham Street Charles could look over 'dust-heaps and dock-leaves and fields . . . at the cupola of St Paul's looming through the smoke'.

Charles, a naturally fastidious boy, was more conscious of the dust-heaps than of the fields, offended after the country cleanliness of Chatham by his neighbours' 'propensity to throw any little trifles they were not in want of into the road, which not only made it rank and sloppy, but untidy, too, on account of the cabbage-leaves'. He noted with disapproval that one of these neighbours was a washerwoman and another a Bow Street Runner, but omitted to observe that the district was an artistic colony such as Chelsea later became. Leigh Hunt had only two years previously left Kentish Town to join Byron and Shelley in Italy. In Bayham Street itself lived Francis Engleheart and William Holl, noted engravers, and the now forgotten dramatist Angelo Selous. To Charles it was a street of failures, to be commemorated for ever as the home of Mr Micawber, that impecunious gentleman drawn from his own father.

It must have been a relief to be taken out for a visit to his godfather, Christopher Huffam (whose name had been wrongly given at the font to Charles as Huffham). * He was a rigger in the Navy, and lived in a pleasant Georgian house, 5 Church Row, Limehouse. The district was then one of romance unspoiled by industry, highly congenial to a boy from Chatham. Its appearance can be re-created by a visit to the older streets of Greenwich. Sailors who had served with Nelson were to be seen, coloured faces (then so rare in London) abounded, a smell of tar and river-water prevailed; and Captain Cuttle became a gleam in his creator's eye. 'It was always,' said Forster, 'a great treat to him to go to Mr Huffham's; and the London night-sights as he returned were a perpetual joy and marvel. Here, too, the comic-singing accomplishment was brought into play so greatly to the admiration of one of the godfather's guests, an honest boat-builder, that he pronounced the little lad to be a "progidy".'

Another relative, Uncle Thomas Barrow, lived in Gerrard Street, Soho, behind Leicester Square, in the top part of a house kept by the widow of a bookseller. Dickens sent the lawyer Jaggers to live there, in *Great Expectations*, in 'rather a stately house of

* There was a Huffham's Staveyard near Jacob's Island which may or may not have belonged to him.

its kind, but dolefully in want of painting, and with dirty windows'. The kindly owner, Mrs Manson, who carried on her late husband's business downstairs, used to lend young Charles books when he passed through the shop: one of them impressed him so much by its description of Covent Garden, which he had never seen, that he ventured to the famous market and snuffed up 'the flavour of the faded cabbage-leaves as if it were the very breath of comic fiction'.

Uncle Thomas, who at this time was laid up with a broken leg, 'was shaved by a very odd old barber out of Dean Street, Soho, who was never tired of reviewing the events of the last war, and especially of detecting Napoleon's mistakes, and rearranging his whole life for him on a plan of his own'. Soho was full of foreigners, artists and writers. Shelley had lived in Poland Street; Thornhill, who painted the dome of St Paul's, in Dean Street; Angelica Kauffman's home was in Golden Square, Hazlitt's in Dean Street. It must have been a stimulating neighbourhood to a young mind like a photographic plate.

Soon the Dickenses left Bayham Street for 4 Gower Street North, where Mrs Dickens proposed to set up a school. Demolished in 1895, it was said to have been a largish six-roomed house with a basement kitchen. It was not their home for long; the school did not attract any pupils, though Charles had to wear out his shoe-leather tramping round the streets with circulars advertising it. Mrs Dickens hoped that Christopher Huffam's East Indian connections would bring her the daughters of wealthy merchants to educate. Unfortunately, the general trade depression of 1824 rendered Huffam bankrupt, and her hopes were gone. Worse was to come: in February 1824 John Dickens was arrested for debt.

At first he seems to have been imprisoned in the King's Bench, across London Bridge in the Borough High Street, at the corner of Borough Road.* It was described by a London historian in 1828

* Biographers have differed about this, some averring that Dickens deliberately put Micawber into the King's Bench rather than the Marshalsea 'that old memories should not be revived', although he had not the least scruple about reviving them when it came to *Little Dorrit*. According to Robert Langton in *The Childhood and Youth of Charles Dickens*, a Mr Dorrett, also of Rochester, was a prisoner for debt in the King's Bench when John Dickens was first imprisoned. Walter Bray, in *Nicholas Nickleby*, lives within the Rules of the Bench, and the description of Horace Kinch, the King's Bench prisoner of the essay 'Night Walks' (in *The Uncommercial Traveller*), has a note of bitterness often associated

22

as 'the most desirable place of incarceration for debtors in England'. These unfortunates might have leave of absence for a day by paying a fee of 4s. 2d., for a second day 3s. 10d. If they had certain means, they were allowed to live in the 'Rules' of the Bench, in lodgings which were dotted about the Borough streets. Only ten years before one of these privileged debtors had been Emma, Lady Hamilton, still lovely in her sad middle-age, gallantly holding parties in her sordid lodging and retaining in her reduced household a music-teacher for Nelson's daughter. A year before the painter Haydon had found the prison itself not too unendurable, leaving his fellow-prisoners with regret. There was a tap-room where drinks could be had, a wine-room for those with more elevated tastes, and a market. That celebrated prisoner Mr Micawber, though remarking on arrest that 'the God of Day had now gone down upon him', managed to enjoy himself in the King's Bench with all his ebullient heart. He was, of course, John Dickens in thin disguise. But to John Dickens's son it was Golgotha, a place of skulls. He would have rejoiced to see its demolition in 1880, if he could have lived so long.

The next prison to which John Dickens was transferred was the Marshalsea, in the Borough High Street. Surprisingly, enough of it has survived to show the character of the whole. Across the street running alongside St George's Church, Southwark, is a high iron railing; behind it, a public garden, once the burial-ground. A great brick vault, smothered in creeper, has been left standing, huge enough and sinister enough to contain the remains of Mrs Sapsea and of a strangled, lime-consumed Edwin Drood. It is large above the common run of vaults, and must have attracted a speculative look from the boy brought up on Mary Weller's ghost stories. Semi-legible, crumbling tombstones are ranged up against the high wall of a derelict building which runs along the north side of the garden. It is all that remains of the Marshalsea, that 'oblong pile of barrack building, partitioned into squalid houses standing back to back, environed by a narrow paved yard, hemmed in by high walls, duly spiked on top'.

Southwark has not forgotten Dickens. The present authors,

---

with Dickens's references to his father. It is all inference rather than evidence, but the King's Bench does seem to have been on Dickens's list of 'haunts'.

hovering about the padlocked gate of the garden, were approached briskly by the inhabitant of a nearby flat. 'You looking at that old place? That's the Marshalsea. You're in Dickens-land now, you know!' and, pointing to a barred window, almost obscured with ivy, 'That's Little Dorrit's window, where she used to sit'. There is a commemorative plaque below it, placed there long ago to tell the traveller that this is the very Marshalsea of Charles Dickens; but the natives need no such reminder. When the gate is opened they can stroll in from the noise of the High Street and sit or stroll on the grass, where Dickens's little town sparrows 'playing at country' importune the passer-by for crumbs, and the blank eyes of the prison windows look down. The last prisoner left it in 1842; in 1887 it became a factory. Now it is a literary memorial, and a bastion to one of London's pleasantly melancholy playgrounds. Many Marshalsea prisoners were buried there, among them Edward Cocker, of arithmetic fame, and Edmund Bonner, Bishop of London in the time of Mary Tudor, who was denied by Elizabeth the First the privilege of kissing her hand, so black was his record of torture and burning in her sister's reign. They buried him in St George's churchyard at midnight, to avoid interruptions from the indignant folk of Southwark. And, strolling among the tombs, Dickens could have read that sad epitaph quoted from Pope's 'Elegy to the Memory of an Unfortunate Lady':

> How Lov'd, how Valued Once, avails thee not!
> To whom related or by whom begot.
> A heap of Dust alone remains of thee;
> 'Tis all thou art, and all the Proud shall be.

A little way up the Borough High Street is the one remaining wing of the old George Inn, its galleries looking down at a yard such as the one at the vanished White Hart, in which took place the meeting between Mr Pickwick and Sam Weller. But Dickens only mentions the George once, in *Little Dorrit*.

The Borough High Street has kept many of its old buildings and something of its old character, overshadowed though it is now by the giant blocks which have risen on the site of old London Bridge station. It is not difficult on a summer evening, when the workers have gone home, to follow the lonely boy down the High Street and across the road to his lodging in Lant Street where, now that his mother and the other children were living in two rooms in the Gower Street house, before joining his father in prison, he occupied 'a back attic . . . at the house of an insolvent court agent. The little window had a pleasant prospect of a timber yard, and when I took possession of my new abode I thought it was a Paradise'. Looking back at his stay there, when he was installing Mr Bob Sawyer in the same lodging, he observed: 'If a man wished to abstract himself from the world—to remove himself from within the reach of temptation—to place himself beyond the possibility of any inducement to look out of the window—he should by all means go to Lant Street.' A drawing of the street in 1888 shows that his estimate was a pretty fair one; the only temptation the shabby, tumbledown street has to offer would seem to be a glass of Porter's Fine Ales in a pub from which a sad young Eliza Doolittle of a mother is emerging, her baby wrapped in her shawl. All trace of the buildings of Dickens's day have gone from Lant Street; only the Charles Dickens Primary School, built in 1877 on the site of his lodging, remains as a reminder of his presence.

There were some pleasures attached to life in the Borough: no bright twelve-year-old could have resisted the travelling fair which came round on Saturday nights, with its attractions of a Fat Pig, a Wild Indian and a Little Lady. There was also a certain magnificence, at such an age, about being able to go into Johnson's alamode beef-house in Clare-Court, Drury Lane, and to order a plate of alamode beef, or to fill oneself up with the stale pastry offered for half-price outside the doors of Tottenham Court Road confectioners, or 'a stout hale pudding, heavy and flabby, with great raisins in it', on sale at a shop in the Strand, near Buckingham Street. Something like the modern coffee-bar was to be found in most central London streets at that time, in which a boy might refresh himself with 'half-a-pint of coffee and a slice of bread and butter'; one was in Maiden Lane and one in St Martin's Lane, somewhere about the site of the Coliseum. On its door was an oval glass plate, with COFFEE ROOM painted on it, which Charles used to gaze at longingly when he had no money for coffee, and which gave him one of the small wounds that were never to heal. 'If I ever find myself in a very different kind of coffee-room now, but where there is such an inscription on glass, and read it backward on the wrong side MOOR EEFFOC (as I often used to do then, in a dismal reverie) a shock goes through my blood.'

25

He had six shillings a week to live on, earned by his own hands. There was in those days no compulsory education; a debtor's child must work. Much has been written of Warren's Blacking Factory, where Charles Dickens suffered an experience which affected him for life. Another child might have passed through it unscathed: after all, it only lasted a few months. But he, so small and slender, was already a genius. He was the Inimitable, the name given to him by his schoolmaster William Giles. The humiliation of menial employment, on view to the public, the deprivation of that schooling which had meant so much to him, and the conviction that his mother had rejected him, impressed themselves on his brain so that he could never forget those months when he sat, cross-legged, sticking labels on to blacking bottles. One of these labels, which were the only trade-marks of the time, showed a bristling cat backing away from its own reflection in a Wellington boot polished to a nicety by Warren's Blacking. It may be a coincidence that Dickens hardly mentions cats in his novels.*

He wrote often and bitterly of this period of his life, in *David Copperfield* and elsewhere. The friend of his later years, Longfellow, spoke in verse what Dickens so often attempted to say in prose, but could not wholly, for his feelings were too deep.

> *There are things of which I may not speak;*
> *There are dreams that cannot die;*
> *There are thoughts that make the strong heart weak,*
> *And a mist before the eye.*
> *And the words of that fatal song*
> *Come o'er me like a chill;*
> *'A boy's will is the wind's will,*
> *And the thoughts of youth are long, long thoughts'.*

Quite apart from the psychological implications of Charles Dickens's employment there, Warren's Blacking Factory was not a pleasant place. George Lamert, cousin of James, had started it in opposition to the older-established business at 30 Strand, begun by Jonathan Warren, who had offered the Lamerts the opportunity of joining his firm and was justifiably aggrieved when they and Robert Warren took themselves and his own cherished

---

* In the Phiz illustration of the scene in *Bleak House* following Mr Krook's death by Spontaneous Combustion, the terrified cat, Lady Jane, is almost the duplicate in reverse of the cat in Warren's advertisement.

blacking recipe to other premises. The rival warehouse (in which even Jonathan's advertisements were pirated) was at 30 Hungerford Stairs, on a site now occupied by the Victoria Embankment Gardens, hard by Charing Cross station.

Dickens described the factory as 'a crazy tumble-down house, abutting of course on the river, and literally overrun with rats. Its wainscotted rooms, and its rotten floors and staircase, and the old grey rats swarming down in the cellars, and the sound of their squeaking and scuffling coming up the stairs at all times, and the dirt and decay of the place, rise up visibly before me, as if I were there again'. This building may well have imbued Dickens with an early distaste for ancient properties. In 1824 few but learned antiquarians were interested in such places; there were no societies for the preservation of anywhere, no buildings scheduled as of architectural and historic interest. The blacking factory, as shown in a contemporary print, appears to our eyes a comely enough building of the early eighteenth century, with bottle-glass windows, one of them a charming bow. It seems to have been converted to industrial use from a private house, probably lived in by a merchant. But because it was old, nobody thought it worth repairing. It was allowed to fall to pieces, attacked by rising damp, for there were no damp-courses, and the river flowed at its feet, by subsidence, extensive dry rot with its peculiarly musty smell, by woodworm and death-watch beetle. Its sanitation was nil. The sewer which had been constructed under the Strand in 1802 discharged its contents into the Thames, whose waters were anything but fragrant, though not as noxious as they became when main drainage was introduced in 1865. The presence of rats was not considered particularly remarkable in such a building, nor was anything done to get rid of them apart from some occasional pistol practice by the boys, or the putting down of poison which caused the rats to die in strychnine agonies under the floor-boards, where their bodies slowly decayed, like that of the cat in *Stalky and Co.*, 'stealing on the air rather as a pale-blue sensation than as any poignant offence. But,' adds Kipling, and his words are relative to young Dickens, 'the mere adumbration of an odour is enough for the sensitive nose and clean tongue of youth'. The Dickenses had never lived in grand style, but their houses or lodgings had always been well-kept and respectable. Some of Charles's loathing of his place of work may well have been based

27

on sheer physical disgust. No wonder that when Joe Gargery of *Great Expectations* came up to London to see the 'Blacking Ware'us' he found that it did not resemble its likeness on the advertisements, where it was 'drawd too architectooralooral'.

The folk of the London streets traversed by the boy on his way to visit his family every night were rich stuff for a future novelist's mental notebook. He went in to see the travelling fair in the show-van with 'a very motley assemblage'. He wandered about, 'so young and childish', among prostitutes, criminals, beggars. Looking back he realized that 'but for the mercy of God, I might easily have been, for any care that was taken of me, a little robber or a little vagabond'. The vanished Adelphi arches, so near the warehouse, were 'a subterranean stable-haunted spot'; he might have said 'a subterranean villain-haunted spot'. A walk through present-day Hungerford Lane on a dark night, or through the arches connecting Villiers Street with Craven Street, will give some faint idea of the ambience of those places and of the sights the boy must have seen. He tells us in *Household Words* how 'I wandered about the City, like a child in a dream, staring at the British merchants, and inspired by a mighty faith in the marvellousness of everything': in other words, protected by innocence, as he was when he visited the theatre in Goodman's Fields where the gallery was populated by sailors and 'others of the lowest description, and their conversation was not improving. But I understood little or nothing of what was bad in it then, and it had no depraving influence on me'. He saw sights in the Marshalsea more revolting than anything which found its way into the chronicle of Mr Pickwick's imprisonment there. He travelled, like Nicholas Nickleby, through a London 'strange in its glooms and flaring lights' (gas had first been used in the streets in 1810, and had a wildly flickering effect completely unlike the steady blaze of electricity). Light fascinated him as much as darkness. 'The rags of the squalid ballad-singer fluttered in the rich light that showed the goldsmith's treasures, pale and pinched-up faces hovered about the windows where was tempting food . . . half-naked shivering figures stopped to gaze at Chinese shawls and golden stuffs of India.'

In districts which are to us only associated with smug commerce, 'wild visions of wickedness, want and beggary' troubled him. Where Trafalgar Square now extends itself, and tourists feed the pigeons, was a sprawl of stables and mews, left over from the ancient Palace of Whitehall. In place of the sweep of Aldwych and the broad ribbon of Kingsway, where classical and mythological figures recline on large clean buildings of which Bush House is typical, a warren of slummy streets ran riot. Dickens's passion for theatres would not have drawn his steps towards Shaftesbury Avenue, for it did not exist. Tottenham Court Road, which became rural at its north end, had its beginnings in the notorious 'Rookery' of St Giles, from which Hogarth had drawn his Gin Lane. Glimpses of the streets Dickens knew may still be seen; Monmouth Street and one side of Lisle Street, the little streets round Fitzroy Square, and a few others which have escaped the redeveloper's attentions. Small Tenterden Street, on the north-east of Hanover Square, has retained no shred of the character it had when young Charles called there to collect his sister Fanny from the Royal Academy of Music. Twentieth-century Oxford Street roars deafeningly just beyond it.

It is a common enough sight today, and one that provokes admiring wonder, to see a tiny child in school uniform, sometimes with an even tinier one by the hand, threading its way with nonchalant professionalism among London traffic, marching intrepidly across seething thoroughfares where adults fear to tread. Just so did Charles's diminutive figure dodge in and out of the path of coaches, gigs, phaetons, wagons and horsemen. He had, with the adaptability of children, become a Cockney. Though his soul was tender, his brain and senses were knife-sharp (Mr Murdstone was to allude to David Copperfield as Brooks of Sheffield), and he was, though the fact is sometimes overlooked, a Georgian, not a Victorian, accustomed to plain speaking and coarse manners, taken from infancy to lyings-in and layings-out. With his inborn gift for mimicry he could imitate any character of street, fair, or booth. 'Walk up, walk up, ladies and gentlemen! Come, my lucky little rogues, and try your fortune for a ha'penny, all prizes and no blanks, a faint heart never wins fair lady!' Or the sailor at the Goodman's Fields Theatre, calling out for the fiddlers and *Rule, Britannia*, and comparing Othello to the black ship's cook in his white nightcap, with a great deal of damning his own and other people's eyes. Or the medical student roistering back to his lodging in St Thomas's Street, Southwark, roaring out a ballad of Bacchus's blisses and Venus's kisses, and this, boys,

29

O this is a bachelor's life. Like a young parrot, Charles registered every intonation and reproduced it faithfully, down to the Cockney's v for w and w for v.

No law concerning children on licensed premises forbade Charles to go into a public-house by himself and order an alcoholic drink. One of his favourite pubs was the little Fox-under-the-Hill, in the Adelphi, approached by an underground passage which once led to the starting-point of the 'half-penny boats'. It vanished with the building of the Embankment. He had a kind of visionary memory, in later life, of sitting eating something on the bench outside, one fine evening, and looking at some coal-heavers dancing before the house. And, on another fine evening, when out on an errand for his father, he called at a public house in Parliament Street, and requested a glass of the VERY best ale. Used as they were to all sorts of customers, the kindly landlord and his wife were a little puzzled by this one, and asked him 'all sorts of questions'. He got his ale, 'though I suspect', he confided to Forster, 'it was not the strongest on the premises; and the land-lord's wife, opening the little half-door and bending down, gave me a kiss that was half-admiring and half-compassionate, but all womanly and good, I am sure'. The pub was the Red Lion at 48 Parliament Street, and it is still there today: not the same building, but a later Victorian one. The old rampant Red Lion sign still rears above the Whitehall traffic (apparently trying either to fly or to climb up the wall) and the building is adorned with a head of Dickens.

While Charles was still employed at the blacking factory its premises were removed to a rather more salubrious spot, north of the Strand, at the corner of Bedford Street and Chandos Street. On the opposite corner stood the White Swan Tavern, where, said Dickens, 'I got my ale, under these new circumstances. The stones in the street may be smoothed by my small feet going across to it at dinner-time, and back again'. On the site of the White Swan there stands today the publishing house of J. M. Dent and Sons Ltd, from which Dickens's works have emanated in the familiar bindings of Everyman's Library. The book-filled windows look across to the spot where once a shame-filled little boy sat publicly displayed at his employment of tying up blacking-pots: 'So brisk at it, that the people used to stop and look in.'

Some time in the summer of 1824 his ordeal was over. John

Dickens was released from prison and the family were reunited in the familiar surroundings of Camden Town, first at an address unknown, then at 'a very small house in a street leading out of Seymour Street'. But the damage had been done. Until old Hungerford Market was pulled down, and old Hungerford Stairs and the rotting old house were destroyed, Dickens never had the courage to go near them, either as youth or man. 'It was a very long time before I liked to go up Chandos Street. My old way home by the Borough made me cry, after my eldest child could speak.'

4

Clerkship and Courtship

No shadows of the past kept Dickens from revisiting the London school he had attended between the ages of twelve and fifteen. He was, indeed, sorry to find it altered. 'We went to look at it, only this last Midsummer, and found that the Railway had cut it up root and branch. A great trunk-line had swallowed the playground, sliced away the schoolroom, and pared off the corner of the house: which, thus curtailed of its proportions, presented itself, in a green stage of stucco, profile-wise towards the road, like a forlorn flat-iron without a handle, standing on end.'

In fact, the house, which stood until two or three years ago on the corner of Hampstead Road and Granby Terrace, had once been a pleasing, ordinary four-storeyed building at the end of a small, graceful row. But by then it was past repair, a gaunt derelict, with a heap of rubble behind the smashed garden wall and rags pinned drunkenly up at the smashed windows. Its demolition came almost as a relief to Dickens-lovers, as death is welcomed by the relatives of a mortally sick person. The plaque placed on it by the former St Pancras Dickens Fellowship was illegible; the fellowship had not been allowed access to clean it. The house at the opposite end of the terrace, where Dickens's friend and illustrator George Cruik-shank lived and died, seemed threatened at one time with the same fate, but when last seen had been repainted and looked in a fair way to survive a little longer the avalanche of cement which is sweeping down on Mornington Crescent.

The school was called Wellington House Academy, sometimes advertised as Mr Jones's Classical Academy. It was 'a school of some celebrity in the neighbourhood'. Dickens was happy there and got on quickly, now that education had been restored to him. He describes Mr Jones, the headmaster, as ignorant and brutal: 'the only branches of education with which he showed the least acquaintance were ruling and corporally punishing. He was always ruling ciphering-books with a bloated mahogany ruler, or smiting the palms of offenders with the same diabolical instrument, or viciously drawing a pair of pantaloons tight with one of his large hands, and caning the wearer with the other.' Dickens's school-fellows confirmed his opinion: 'a Welshman; a most ignorant fellow, and a mere tyrant,' said Dr Henry Danson, but did not feel that Dickens himself had had much to complain about: 'I do not think he came in for any of Mr Jones's scourging propensity; in fact, together with myself, he was only a day-pupil, and with these there was a wholesome fear of tales being carried home to the parents.' This did not prevent Dickens from drawing his old headmaster as the abominable Mr Creakle of *David Copperfield*.

A different light is thrown on Mr Jones by a discovery in 1960. Mr Leslie Staples, then editor of *The Dickensian*, read in a book published in Toronto that somewhere in Old St Pancras church-yard was the tombstone of Dickens's schoolmaster. A search was made, and the stone found, in a dirty and dilapidated state. Cleaned up, the inscription reads:

Sacred to the memory of Mr William Jones, for many years Master of a Respectable School in this Parish, who departed this Life on the 20th day of January, 1836, aged 59 years. The inflexible integrity of his Character and the social and domestic Virtues which adorned his private Life will long be Cherished in the recollection of all those who knew him.

All, presumably, except his pupils. Tombstone eulogies may be taken with a heavy pinch of salt; but at least we now know that Mr Jones had private worries and sleepless nights which may well have exacerbated his fiery Welsh temper, for the stone also commemorates his little daughter, who died 'the 5th day of February 1827, aged 2 years and 2 months'.

Sweet child! thy lingering sufferings now are o'er,
And Angels greet thee on Heavens blissful shore.

The tombstone of the Jones family has been preserved by the efforts of the Dickens Fellowship, and bears a commemorative plaque. It stands near the centre of the beautiful St Pancras Gardens by the ancient church.

Charles's schooling did not last long. John Dickens, though out of prison, was by no means out of debt; he never would be. Unable to pay the fees any more, he took Charles away from Wellington House in April 1827, and moved his family, including the new baby, Augustus, to a lodging in The Polygon, Clarendon Square, Somers Town.* It was necessary for Charles to find a job. In May he became clerk to a firm of solicitors, Ellis and Blackmore, of 5 Holborn Court, Gray's Inn, now 1 South Square. In *David Copperfield* it became the residence of Tommy Traddles. A beautiful building to our eyes, it was, in the memory of one of his colleagues, 'a poor old set of chambers of three rooms, the front overlooking the Court, a room at the back, and the clerk's office which was shut off from the passage by a glass partition'. At the end of 1827 the firm removed to newer chambers at 6 Raymond Buildings, Gray's Inn. But, new or old, the premises seem to have made an indelibly bad impression on Charles's mind. All his life he tilted against the law, its delays, its hypocrisies, its corruptions, all of which were for him epitomized in its physical surroundings. In the essay 'Chambers', from *The Uncommercial Traveller*, he seems to be working off a personal hatred against Gray's Inn: 'I look upon Gray's Inn generally as one of the most depressing institutions in brick and mortar, known to the children of men. Can anything be more dreary than its arid Square, Sahara Desert of the law, with the ugly old tiled-topped tenements, the dirty windows, the bills To Let, To Let, the door-posts inscribed like gravestones, the crazy gateway giving upon the filthy Lane, the scowling, iron-barred prison-like passage into Verulam Buildings, the mouldy red-nosed ticket porters with little coffin-plates . . . the dry, hard, atomy-like appearance of the whole dustheap? When my uncommercial travels tend to this dismal spot, my comfort is in its rickety state. Imagination gloats over the fulness of time when the staircases shall have quite tumbled down—they are daily wearing into an ill-savoured powder, but have not quite tumbled down yet . . . then shall a squalid little

* Clarendon Square is now Chatton Street, Polygon Road, Phoenix Road and Warrington Street. The Polygon has been demolished.

trench, with rank grass and a pump in it, lying between the coffee-house * and South Square, be wholly given up to cats and rats, and not, as now, have its empire divided between those animals and a few briefless bipeds . . . who glance down, with eyes better glazed than their casements, from their dreary and lack-lustre rooms. Then shall the way Nor' Westward, now lying under a short grim colonnade where in summer-time pounce flies from law-stationering windows into the eyes of laymen, be choked with rubbish and happily become impassable. Then shall the gardens where turf, trees and gravel wear a legal livery of black, run rank, and pilgrims go to Gorhambury to see Bacon's effigy as he sat, and not come here (which in truth they seldom do) to see where he walked.'

It is a piece of vituperation worthy of Thersites. Once again it seems that Charles's young sensibilities had been offended by the smells and squalor of old buildings (although Raymond Buildings only dated from 1819). Elsewhere in the essay he distastefully tosses off hints of other nastinesses. The occupant of a top set of chambers, he says, was convinced that they were clean. Dickens was not. 'They were so dirty that I could take off the distinctest impression of my figure on any article of furniture by merely lounging upon it for a few moments; and it used to be a private amusement of mine to print myself off—if I may use the expression —all over the rooms. It was the first large circulation I had. At other times I have accidentally shaken a window-curtain while in animated conversation with Parkle, and struggling insects which were certainly red, and were certainly not ladybirds, have dropped on the back of my hand.'

Fortunately for the twentieth century, Dickens's vindictive prophecy for Gray's Inn has not yet come true. The chambers where he worked are still in existence; the staircases have not crumbled. The Inn is a refuge of beauty and peace for the workers of Holborn, who stroll and sit in its gardens in their lunch-hour, whose eyes are rested by the calm elegance of its seventeenth- and eighteenth-century houses. Consulting one's solicitor in Raymond Buildings, one may turn from legal documents to a refreshing vision of lovely green, the Elizabethan gardens at the back, the neat walk at the front; everywhere are trees and mellow

* The Gray's Inn Coffee House, where David Copperfield stayed when he visited Tommy Traddles.

brick. The staircases are dark, indeed, the sanitary arrangements of at least one set of chambers known to the present authors probably not much improvement on those of a century ago, but the charms of antiquity, to which Dickens was immune, make them excusable. If squalor, cats and rats once dominated the place, they have been banished long ago; but it is difficult to believe that they were ever quite so bad as Dickens painted them. As William Kent * so shrewdly said of him: 'He would have turned the scythe upon Father Time himself.'

Gray's was only one of the Inns of Court to attract his savage criticism. One and all, they symbolized for him dirt, death and decay: they 'founded their claim to respectable antiquity upon a good collection of corpses'. From the handsome gateway which is all that remains of Clifford's Inn it is difficult to reconstruct the gruesome episode of the tenant who, oppressed by an uneasy feeling about the closet in his new chambers, smashed the lock with a poker and discovered 'standing bolt upright in the corner, the last tenant, with a little bottle clasped firmly in his hand, and his face livid with the hue of a painful death'. Clement's Inn was rebuilt when the Law Courts replaced older buildings, and no trace remains to substantiate the 'dark Old Bailey whisper concerning Clement's, and importing how the black creature who holds the sun-dial there, was a Negro who slew his master and built the dismal pile out of the contents ôf his strong-box'. Lyon's Inn, with its 'dismallest underground dens', was swept away during the construction of Aldwych. Barnard's has gone, and Furnival's. Most of the others which remain reappear throughout Dickens's novels. Disliking them, he was drawn back to them again and again by that preoccupation with the macabre which characterized the man whose shadows were all the darker for his surpassing brightness.

He was, truth to tell, rather enjoying himself among the lairs of the law in his days as a clerk. His passion for theatres took him to the great playhouses of London, the Haymarket, Drury Lane, and Covent Garden. Fire and reconstruction have changed their faces and their interiors, but Dickens would recognize much of the first two, and find the surroundings of the third little altered; it is still approached through the great market where he gazed

* in *London for Dickens Lovers.*

wistfully at the fruit he could not buy, and snuffed up simultaneously the flavour of comedy and cabbage-leaves. Astley's Amphitheatre—'Dear, dear, what a place it looked that Astley's!' —has gone; it was in Westminster Bridge Road. Sadler's Wells stands on the site to which he would walk, perhaps turning up Gray's Inn Road and passing Bagnigge Wells, in the fields of Clerkenwell. Merely spectating did not satisfy the drama-infatuated youth. To the private theatres, such as those in Catherine Street, Strand, or in Gray's Inn Road (then Gray's Inn Lane), he went with his friend and fellow-clerk Potter and 'not unfrequently engaged in parts'. His essay in *Sketches by Boz* on 'Private Theatres' conveys exuberantly the atmosphere of those raffish places where wistful amateur ambitions for the footlights might find an outlet. Here, in the low comedian, the 'pale bony little girl with the necklace of blue glass beads', the tall stout lady who looked 'a little like Mrs Siddons—at a considerable distance', he found the stuff from which the immortal Crummleses and their talented company in *Nicholas Nickleby* were made.

Sometimes the two boys would cross the river to Vauxhall Gardens, then still a London pleasure-place of 'illuminated groves', now buried beneath a heap of grimy buildings; Vauxhall station stands more or less on its site. Or they would go on the river by pleasure-boat to the same resorts as those enjoyed by voyagers today. Down to pleasant Richmond on 'a Richmond tide' was all very well, but on the return journey the young ladies of the party might be (and frequently were) considerably embarrassed by the 'sportive youths' who were in the habit of bathing in the nude just in front of the Penitentiary on Millbank. The youths, however sportive, would find Thames water curiously unappetizing these days, and the Penitentiary has been replaced by the Tate Gallery.

On Easter Monday 1829, Dickens very probably went to Greenwich Fair; not by river, it seems, but in one of the new omnibuses by a road crammed with horse-traffic of every conceivable kind. 'The dust flies in clouds, ginger-beer corks go off in volleys, the balcony of every public-house is crowded with people . . . half the private houses are turned into tea-shops . . . everybody is anxious to get on, and actuated by the common wish to be at the fair, or in the park, as soon as possible.' On the slopes above the noble buildings of the Royal Naval College and the

Queen's House the boys and their girls would wander, the principal amusement being 'to drag young ladies up the steep hill which leads to the Observatory, and then drag them down again, at the very top of their speed'; or to become 'violently affectionate' on the grass, to the accompaniment of such cries as 'Oh! ha' done, then, George!' The old sailors Dickens loved to see earned a few pence for showing the sights of Greenwich through a telescope. These sights did not include the *Cutty Sark* which now so imperially rules the scene. She would not be built for another forty years, and in any case would have aroused no comment in a river basin crowded with beautiful sail.

By that Easter the young clerk had decided to change his job. He had now made himself master of shorthand, and embarked on what he hoped would lead to a career as a parliamentary reporter. He began by reporting in Doctors' Commons, where the law dealt with matters later taken over by the Probate, Divorce and Admiralty Division of the High Court. Doctors' Commons (the last relics of which were removed by German bombs) was 'a lazy old nook near St Paul's Churchyard . . . where they grant marriage licences to love-sick couples, and divorces to unfaithful ones'.* He did not find either the atmosphere or the work congenial, and was glad enough to leave it to join his father as a reporter for *The Mirror of Parliament* and a new evening newspaper, *The True Sun*.

The Houses of Parliament which are perhaps the most famous of London landmarks today did not then exist. Parliamentary debates took place in part of the old Palace of Westminster, in singularly cramped and uncomfortable conditions. Once again Dickens found himself surrounded by antiquity, and strongly objected to it. Speaking on Administrative Reform in 1855, he looked back contemptuously to the 'worn-out, worm-eaten, rotten old bits of wood' which symbolized for him the state of politics in his youth, the failure of the Reform Bill to become law, the antiquated processes of government which caused so much suffering. He rejoiced over the great fire of 1834 which destroyed

* The only building to survive of Doctors' Commons is the Deanery, Dean's Court, on the south side of Ludgate Hill. At 5 Bell Yard, at the end of Carter Lane, which leads out of Dean's Court, Dickens had an office during his period as a reporter. Visitors to the Mermaid Theatre will find themselves in this vicinity, which is well worth a stroll.

the physical body of the Houses. But even the new ones could not satisfy his lust for progress, enlightenment, advancement in all things. 'The national pig is not nearly over the stile yet; and the little old woman, Britannia, hasn't got home tonight.'

He seems to have had no settled home at this time. In spite of John Dickens's regular earnings, improvidence seems to have driven the family from lodging to lodging. When Charles took out a reader's ticket at the British Museum on his eighteenth birthday in 1830 he gave his address as 10 Norfolk Street, Fitzroy Square. Norfolk Street, running between Goodge Street and Tottenham Street, later became part of Cleveland Street, of which the house became 22. The lodgings were above a shop kept by one John Dodd, who had been there in 1804, and it is probable that the Dickenses had stayed with him then, before John Dickens's transfer to Chatham. The house has escaped the wholesale demolition which has overtaken so much of the district. One may contemplate the handsome Georgian front door through which the young reporter would dash in and out on his way to the House, or a gruelling coach journey. The shop, once Mr Dodd's, bears at the side of it a sign which has a pleasingly Dickensian ring: 'Simkins' Sandwiches'.

The house to which the family next moved has been equally fortunate, when one considers the fate of the southern end of Fitzroy Street. Next to the Yorkshire Grey public house is No. 25, which has remained outwardly unchanged. Somewhere behind its bland façade—perhaps in the first-floor front parlour with the pretty balconied windows—young Dickens wrote to his friends inviting them to come and 'knock up a chaunt or two' and enjoy 'A Glass of Punch and a Cigar'.

In January 1833 the family moved into 18 Bentinck Street, near Portland Place. From this lodging he walked, as he had done from previous ones during the past three years or so, to Lombard Street in the City, where, at No. 2 (replaced by tall buildings in which nobody lives) was the home of George Beadnell, manager of the banking house of Smith, Payne and Smith; the object of Dickens's visits was George Beadnell's daughter, Maria.

The City was then as much residential as commercial. Deserted now after working hours, holding little human life beyond care-takers' families, it is hard to imagine those quiet streets as the home of multitudinous merchants, traders and private individuals.

The first directory, *A Collection of the Names of the Merchants living in and about the City of London*, published in 1677, listed 1,953 business men in the area, a number which must easily have been doubled or trebled by 1830. It was usual for a banker to live in premises adjoining his bank, as did Mr Beadnell. In the first-floor drawing-room which, like so many contemporary houses, probably had folding doors which allowed it to be extended to the full length of the house, many cheerful evening parties were held. The house and the bank have vanished; on the site stand the Scottish Provident Institution buildings. There is not even an echo left of Maria's harp, Anne's lute, Margaret's soprano voice, or of that other voice, a light tenor with a slightly metallic quality, upraised in one of his favourite comic songs:

> *In Gray's Inn, not long ago,*
> *An old maid lived a life of woe;*
> *She vos fifty-three, vith a face like tan,*
> *And she fell in love vith a cats'-meat man.*
> *Oh much she loved this cats'-meat man,*
> *He vos a good-lookin' cats'-meat man,*
> *Her roses and lilies vos turned to tan*
> *Ven she fell in love with the cats'-meat man.*

Sometimes the ballad would be sentimental, for Maria's ears alone. One perhaps, which Mr Feeder would one day murmur to Cornelia Blimber as they danced:

> *Had I a heart for falsehood framed,*
> *I ne'er could injure you!*

A meal of gargantuan proportions would be enjoyed before the music. Dickens improvised a long, curious poem on one such meal, in which each dish was personalized as a member of the company. Maria's parents were, respectively, a sirloin of beef and a rib of the same, her two sisters nice little ducks, Charles himself a young summer cabbage without a heart, for he had lost his to the girl whose dark beauty, charming shape and delicious coquetry prevented him from comparing her to anything but herself. He imagined the whole company dead (a characteristic Dickensian macabrerie), Maria with 'Spring's early flowers strewn over her bier', her small spaniel Daphne clasped to her breast. It was

40

typical of him that his courtship should be conducted in a church-yard, that of St Michael Queenhithe, in Huggin Lane. In later life it would give him a painful pleasure to walk there again, and remember himself at eighteen, sheltering with Maria in the old church: 'and when I said to my Angelica, "Let the blessed event, Angelica, occur at no altar but this!" and when my Angelica consented that it should occur at no other—which it certainly never did, for it never occurred anywhere. And O, Angelica, what has become of you, this present Sunday morning when I can't attend to the Sermon; and, more difficult question than that, what has become of Me as I was when I sat by your side?'

The churchyard remains, but the Wren church, its spire topped by a little ship, was pulled down in 1896; that was what became of it. And of the lovers? Maria was considered too high game for the dandified, Cockneyfied young shorthand writer, more like an actor than a respectable person in his dazzling flowery waistcoats and cheap glittering scarf-pins, his large bright eyes no dimmer than they and his long brown hair flowing on his collar in ringlets almost as long as Maria's own.* Her parents sent her out of his way, to finishing school in France, and when she came back she had changed, as geographical removes can change a person. For a year or so she blew hot and cold, until in the early summer of 1833 the romance was broken, together with his heart. Perhaps it never quite mended again.

He was tired of living with his creditor-hounded parents, and for a time experimented with lodging on his own. But his rooms at Cecil Street, Strand, were most unsatisfactory. The people were bad cooks, slovenly and dirty. He gave them notice and wrote to his friend Henry Kolle in the spring of 1832 that he had not yet fixed on 'a local habitation and a name'.

It must have been a relief to him, in his unhappy, unsettled state (how permanent a state it was to be) to leave the 'gritty' streets of London for a temporary address at North End, Hampstead, where a Mrs Davis, laundress, kept lodgings in the little hamlet below Jack Straw's Castle and the Bull and Bush, on the hill leading down to the open fields of Golders Green and Kilburn. Some of North End's cottages have survived, but there is no knowing in which one Mrs Davis entertained Genius unawares.

* He wore it short during his courtship of Catherine Hogarth.

At Highgate, across the top of the heath, another landlady may have wondered at the strange, mercurial young man whose family moved into her house in the August of that year. He wrote to Kolle from Fitzroy Street: 'As we have had a little sickness among our family we intend going to Highgate for a fortnight. The Spot we have chosen is in a very pleasant Neighbourhood, and I have discovered a green lane which looks as if nature had intended it for a smoking place.

'If you can make it convenient to come down, write to me and fix your own day. I am sorry I cannot offer you a bed because we are so pressed for room that I myself hang out at the Red Lion, but should you be so disposed to stay all Night I have no doubt you can be provided with a bed at the same Establishment.

'The address is "Mrs Goodman's next door to the old Red Lion Highgate."'

The Old Red Lion was so called to distinguish it from another inn, the Red Lion and Sun, a little farther down North Road on the opposite side, towards Highgate Village. They were only two among Highgate's many inns: in 1826 it had nineteen to serve its small village population and the north-bound coach trade and the drovers coming in from the country to Smithfield. At each inn the facetious ceremony of Swearing on the Horns was kept up, an excuse for drinks all round. Candidates were enjoined 'to pledge no man first when a woman is near', 'never to kiss the maid when the mistress was willing', and so forth, kissing the horns at each mock oath. The Red Lion had ram's horns in its ancient, panelled tap-room, a plain Georgian exterior, and little shops as neighbours on the south side. The green lane, so ideal for smoking, may have been Gallows Lane, which ran alongside the present St Michael's School, or Bromwich Walk, almost paralleling West Hill, or the ancient footpath leading from Hampstead Lane across the Spaniards Farm to East Finchley. All have gone, as Highgate's residential desirability has increased. But there remains Swains Lane (once Swines Lane, from its use by the pig-drovers), running down between the Old Hall and St Michael's Church. When Dickens stayed in Highgate the Old Hall, now flats, was a private house, and 'the church with the tall spire' was only just begun. Highgate Cemetery, to our eyes so ancient, a place of mouldering urns and melancholy beauty, was then meadows; even the bright mind, the supernormal awareness of Dickens can hardly have conceived that one day his father, mother, baby daughter and brother would lie there.

Highgate reappears often in his novels, but never so vividly, so lovingly drawn, as in *David Copperfield*. David's Aunt Betsey Trotwood lives in a cottage in 'the Highgate Road', presumably at the foot of West Hill, on the way to Kentish Town; there are many such cottages left, though rendered shabby and humiliated by time and London smoke. On his way up to the village, if he walked from Miss Trotwood's, David would pass on the right the lovely Georgian terrace which stands back from the road in all its original dignified grace. He would recognize West Hill today, still a steep winding lane with pleasant gardens and some of its original houses; and at the top, in the village itself, he might see, still standing, the home to which he brought Dora, his bride.

'Such a beautiful little house as it is, with everything so bright and new; with the flowers on the carpets looking as if freshly gathered, and the green leaves on the paper as if they had just come out; with the spotless muslin curtains, and the blushing rose-coloured furniture, and Dora's garden hat with the blue ribbon—do I remember now, how I loved her in such another hat when I first knew her!—already hanging on its little peg . . . and everybody tumbling over Jip's Pagoda.'

When David and Dora, before their marriage, have finished delightedly inspecting their house, David goes home 'more incredulous than ever, to a lodging that I have hard by'. It is a fair guess that the lodging Dickens had in mind was the Red Lion, from which he had strolled out, his mind full of misery and Maria, past many a 'beautiful little house' in which he could imagine himself and his lost love. Perhaps it was one of the cottages in North Road, which still stand near the Red Lion and Sun, small, trim, more elegant than in his day, still rural in increasingly urban surroundings. He placed the Copperfields' home, later in the same chapter, next door to Miss Trotwood's, with a communicating path between the cottages. However, Phiz's illustration of David, in his sitting-room, hearing the news of Dora's death, shows the spire of St Michael's on the south side of the house, with a boatman rowing on the water which occupied the centre of Pond Square before it was paved later in the century: this would place the cottage somewhere along South Grove, backing on to Pond Square. But the church may merely have been included in the picture so that the cross surmounting its spire might symbolize Agnes's 'solemn hand upraised towards Heaven' as she announces the child-wife's passing.

Dora was all Maria; hers was the blue hat, the little spaniel. The story of Dickens's infatuation for her is chronicled in David's courtship of Dora. With Highgate, in his unhappy twentieth year, the spoiled romance which helped to change his character was identified. In Highgate he became, in essence, David Copperfield. It became to him the piece of London which alone held a piece of his cherished, undisillusioned youth. With unconscious symbolism he placed the home of Steerforth, that double of George Strough-hill, his childhood friend, at what is now called Church House: 'an old brick house at Highgate on the summit of the hill . . . a genteel old-fashioned house, very quiet and orderly. From the windows of my room I saw all London lying in the distance like a great vapour, with here and there some lights twinkling through it.'

London still lies so, over a century and a quarter after. Looking down on her from the crest of Swains Lane, in a certain dusk-light, it is possible to see her as he did, a great vapour pierced with lights, a mystery.

Before August was over he had gone down the hill again, to take up miserably bleak lodgings in Furnival's Inn.

5

'The Last of the Old Coaching Days'

Fortunately for the blighted lover, there was plenty of excitement and activity in his working life, which took him out into the provinces to report elections and political speeches. It left him little time to moon about London. Between 1833 and 1835 he was dashing from town to town, working under incredibly uncomfortable conditions. Towards the end of his life he told journalists at a Press dinner how he 'often transcribed for the printer, from my shorthand notes, important public speeches in which the strictest accuracy was required, and a mistake in which would have been to a young man severely compromising, writing on the palm of my hand, by the light of a dark lantern, in a post-chaise and four, galloping through a wild country, and through the dead of the night, at the then surprising rate of fifteen miles an hour'.

'He saw the last of the old coaching days, and of the old inns that were a part of them', says Forster. Dickens himself has described some of the less romantic aspects of those days, not to be guessed from the countless prints and Christmas cards depicting bright-painted coaches, laden with fair ladies and jolly gentlemen, dashing merrily through idyllic English landscapes. In fact, such a journey would begin by your being compelled to rise by candlelight, at half-past four; to dress yourself by the light of 'the flaring flat candle with the long snuff' (no easy task), after which you left the house as silently as possible, pausing only for a cup of coffee. The question of breakfast does not seem to have arisen.

Out in the street, the brisk frost, you find, has given way to a miserable thaw. 'You look down the long perspective of Oxford Street, the gas-lights mournfully reflected on the wet pavement, and can discern no speck in the road to encourage the belief that there is a cab or a coach to be had—the very coachmen have gone home in despair.' Those who look in vain for a taxi on a wet day in Oxford Street now, with a train to catch, will appreciate Dickens's feelings. In spite of the terrible weather conditions, he tells us, you trudge on, surrounded by falling cart-horses, milk-women with list tied round their shoes to keep them from slipping, shop-boys crying with cold on their master's doorsteps. But at last you arrive at the Golden Cross Inn. This great coaching-house, as Dickens knew it, stood somewhere about the site of Nelson's Column. In his reporting days it was faced with demolition, for Trafalgar Square was about to replace the old King's Mews and the area south of St Martin's Lane which was so famous for its little eating-houses that it was known as Porridge Island. (It was here that young Charles had thirstily studied the mystic sign MOOR EEFFOC). A handsome, pinnacled and castellated building it appears in old prints, but David Copperfield impatiently dismisses it as 'a mouldy sort of establishment in a close neighbourhood'. There is, of course, no sign in the coach-yard of the Birmingham High-Flyer; but it is 'up the yard', you are told, and there is a quarter of an hour's grace in which you may repair to the taproom, 'not with any absurd idea of warming yourself, because you feel such a result to be utterly hopeless, but for the purpose of procuring some hot brandy-and-water, which you do —when the kettle boils! an event which occurs exactly two minutes and a half before the time fixed for the starting of the coach'.

So, breakfastless, you join your cold, peevish fellow-passengers either in the straw-flavoured stuffiness of the coach interior, or (unimaginably to us) as an Outside, perched in what appears to our eyes to be great insecurity on the top. The nightmare journey begins; such a one as is described in the fifth chapter of *Nicholas Nickleby*. As ever, Dickens spares us the more painful details. There are recorded instances of outside passengers, particularly children, dying of cold and exposure. Coach-sickness must have been a frequent occurrence. Those who are forced to travel on a Sunday, in this day and age, by relics of British Rail's old rolling

46

stock, with its quaint absence of corridors, will even on a short journey comprehend with horror the thought of a coach-ride from London to York under the same conditions. The hurried stops at posting-inns can barely have sufficed for the needs of a load of passengers, and the 'conveniences' offered, in the form of one or two earth-privies, defy imagination. Perhaps Dickens was right to leave them out.

Yet there must have been to the young reporter more than a little exhilaration in these journeys. He loved speed, he loved change of scene, he loved to have his immense capacities for application stretched to their full limit. His travels in the provinces gave him immeasurable material for the books he had yet to write. Most of his impressions found early outlet in *The Pickwick Papers*. In Edinburgh, reporting Lord Grey, he collected the notion for the Bagman's Uncle's tale of the ghostly coach. The Suffolk elections at Ipswich and Sudbury in 1835 supplied him with Eatanswill, its Buffs and Blues; in Birmingham Mr Winkle, Senior, would live; in Bristol his future daughter-in-law, Arabella Allen, would languish in the care of an aunt, and Sam Weller would court the pretty housemaid. Ipswich would see Mr Peter Magnus fussing over the brown paper parcel and the striped hat-box, and Mr Pickwick in horrified occupation of the wrong bed-room. Bath would provide the world with Angelo Cyrus Bantam, Esq., with the ever-memorable footmen's Swarry, and with Mr Winkle's dreadful experience at Royal Crescent. At an ancient inn on Marlborough Downs Tom Smart would take an antique chair's advice on the conduct of his love-affair.

Scenes for other books were forming in his mind. Leamington and Warwick awaited 'Cleopatra' Skewton and the fateful first meeting of her proud daughter with the prouder Dombey. The George at Amesbury (or was it the Green Dragon at Alderbury?) had only a few years to wait for Mark Tapley and rose-blooming Mrs Lupin. His memory was a living Panorama, that continuous revolving landscape so popular with his contemporaries. Everything he saw was photographed upon it, as the sun-picture with which the painter Daguerre was already experimenting recorded images upon silver iodide.

It is, of course, impossible to see Dickens's England today, as he saw it from stage-coach and post-chaise. Only here and there have the roads he took survived in anything like the appearance

47

they had before the railways, and industrialism, and building development laid an ugly veil over the face of England. But before the coming of the motorways it was at least possible to glimpse it, given certain conditions. You would travel by coach; by motor-coach, large, warm, luxurious to a degree inconceivable to travellers in the days of William IV. It would start from Victoria, a name of no significance to that very young Dickens, and would leave the coach-station at some late hour of night—eleven, perhaps. Its route through London would not be markedly Dickensian in aspect; but as it progressed northwards the journey would take you back further, ever further, towards the journey made by long-dead passengers in vehicles long ago turned to dust and match-wood. The Great North Road has its source, so to speak, in Highgate Village, a place little changed, once the lamps are out, from the one that Dickens wandered, smoking his cigar in the green lanes and thinking of Maria. The great posting-inns are there still, and all along the route: the Old Crown on Highgate Hill, where the horses were halted before their hearts and lungs were exhausted; the Angel where the traitor Simon Lovat had halted in 1746 on his way to the Tower and the block; the Gatehouse where a cross and sleepy toll-keeper had to be knocked up to take his due. Farther north, the Bald-Faced Stag at East Finchley, the Tally-ho beyond it, the Old Red Lion crouching at the foot of Barnet Hill, and the New Red Lion (only it was not so very new, for Pepys had drunk there) at the top; and so on to St Albans, sleeping in the moonlight, and soon after the first pause for refreshment at an inn where Dickens's coach, too, would have paused. Hitchin, Baldock, all the villages and little towns on the way seemed depopulated, shrunken to their semblance of a century and more ago. One saw England, as Dickens saw the plot of *Edwin Drood* unravelling, 'by a kind of backward light'.

He was not only a reporter, on his later parliamentary journeys, but an author, though a very tentative one. One evening, at twilight, he dropped the manuscript of a short story, 'A Dinner at Poplar Walk', 'with fear and trembling, into a dark letter-box up a dark court in Fleet Street'. It was the letter-box of the *Monthly Magazine*. The editor published the story, to its author's tearful joy, and asked for more. *Sketches by Boz* had come into being, though they were not published as a collection until the following year, 1834, when they appeared as *Sketches of London Scenes and Characters*.

The sketches drew for their material upon the people and, in particular, the places Dickens had been avidly studying throughout his twenty-one years of life. Chatham and Rochester were there, disguised as 'Mudfog', and 'Dullborough' and 'Great Winglebury': the neighbours at Ordnance Terrace appeared and the London of his childhood and youth poured out in print—Doctors' Commons, Seven Dials, the streets at night and in the morning, Greenwich Fair and the private theatres and Vauxhall and Astley's, the gin-shops, pawnbrokers' and prisons, the old coaches and the new omnibuses, the pleasures of the river. He did not mention the blacking factory, or the dismal lodgings in which his family lurked.

Early in 1835 he was living away from them, at 13 Furnival's Inn, proposing to his friend Henry Austin that they might share his chambers there. In *Martin Chuzzlewit* the Inn was 'a shady, quiet place echoing to the footsteps of the stragglers who have business there; and rather monotonous and gloomy on summer evenings'. Perhaps this was the reason why he desired Austin's company.

His young brother Fred shared the chambers, but presumably paid nothing towards the rent. In *Edwin Drood* Furnival's was the refuge of Rosa, when she flew to Mr Grewgious from the hateful wooing of John Jasper, and was accommodated in a room 'airy, clean, comfortable, almost gay', in the care of an Unlimited head chambermaid. Evidently this Inn of Court was less repulsive to Dickens than the others: it has gone now, and the singularly hideous Prudential Insurance building has risen instead. But somewhere in the summer of 1835 he removed, this time to a district new to him, far from Marylebone and Holborn. His new lodging was at 18 Selwood Place, Queen's Elm, Brompton, just off the Fulham Road; he chose it because two hundred yards away was 18 York Place, the home of Mr George Hogarth.

Like Mr Beadnell, Mr Hogarth, the Scottish editor of the *Evening Chronicle*, was blessed with attractive daughters. Dickens's first visits to him were occasioned by Hogarth's sponsorship of the *Sketches by Boz*, but before long the object of them was clearly Catherine Hogarth, the eldest daughter. She was a plump, rosy girl, 'with the large heavy-lidded blue eyes so much admired by men', said a friend: that the eyes had a sleepy look and the chin was weak did not trouble Dickens at all. He swiftly persuaded himself that he was in love with her. She was not of Maria's teasing, coquettish nature, and he was determined that she should not treat him as badly as Maria had done. Any 'coldness', 'capricious restlessness', or 'sullen and inflexible obstinacy' manifested by his beloved drew a sharp, almost paternally pompous, reproof from him. In spite of these ominous symptoms, there were many gay, amorous evenings at the pleasant, rather raffish house in residential Brompton, where gardens and orchards flourished and no mammoth shadow of the great museums yet darkened the semi-rural scene. Dickens could not get rid of the lease of 13 Furnival's Inn until the end of 1835. Then he gave it up, for he and 'dearest Kate', otherwise known as Pig, Wig, Mouse or Tatie, were to be married in the spring, and No. 13 would not suit as a matrimonial home, having no kitchen and banning children from its precincts.

House-hunting, like betrothal, was a new experience. In November 1835, Dickens was writing to Kate: 'I strolled about Pentonville ... and looked at one or two houses in the new streets. They are extremely dear, the cheapest I looked at being £55 a year with taxes. Their situation for business is undeniable certainly, and the houses themselves are very pretty, but this is too much.'

The houses he was inspecting can still be seen in and around the Pentonville Road, between King's Cross and the Angel. Grimy, put to comparatively base uses, they are still pretty, and in areas like Myddleton Square have become fashionable residences once more. When Dickens wrote *Oliver Twist* he put the estimable Mr Brownlow into 'a neat house, in a quiet shady street near Pentonville', making of a district with pleasant association a refuge for an ill-treated child, poor Oliver. It was a trick he was to perform again and again.

Such commitments as a visit to Newgate and a trip to Hatfield interrupted his search. From the Salisbury Arms at Hatfield he told Kate that he was 'waiting until the remains of the Marchioness of Salisbury are dug from the ruins of her Ancestor's Castle ... the Inquest ... cannot be held until the bones (if the fire has left any) are discovered'. One may imagine him thoroughly enjoying this gruesome vigil, without the slightest regret, or even awareness, that the disastrous fire in which the 85-year-old Marchioness died had also destroyed the west wing of the Cecils' noble house, one of the most historic of English buildings. The incident served him as another ingredient of *Oliver Twist*: Bill Sikes escapes momentarily from the vision of the murdered Nancy's eyes by helping to fight the fire. 'In every part of that great fire was he; but he bore a charmed life, and had neither scratch nor bruise, nor weariness nor thought, till morning dawned again, and only smoke and blackened ruins remained.'

Amidst all his scurryings up and down (he writes to Kate from Kettering and Northampton in December 1835) he received an offer from the publishers Chapman and Hall to write a serial for publication in monthly parts. It was to deal with the humorous misadventures of a group of Cockney sportsmen, and was to be no more than an extended set of captions for drawings by the comic artist Robert Seymour. The first spark had been ignited of the glorious blaze that would be *The Pickwick Papers*. Significantly, Dickens uses much in this period the word 'flare' to describe anything from an election row to a party. Fire and light and shadow, of which he was himself all compounded, were constantly to recur in his descriptions and metaphors.

In February he moved into what was to be his first married home. He was back in Furnival's Inn, this time at No. 15: 'three-pair front, south, at £50 a year for three years certain'. The chambers consisted of three rooms on the third floor, with a kitchen in the basement and permission (presumably) to have as many children in them as might reasonably be produced during a three-year lease. Really intended for bachelor use, they were perfectly suitable for a married couple, particularly when furnished with the decanters, jugs, lustres, and 'magnificent china Jars' which the bridegroom considered essential fittings.

He married Kate at the handsome new church of St Luke's, Chelsea, on 2nd April 1836. This church was chosen, presumably, because of its closeness to the bride's home, where the wedding-breakfast was held, but it was also appropriate to a bridegroom who held old churches in such disfavour. St Luke's has mellowed since its building in 1820 into a pleasant piece of early Gothic. After the wedding, says Forster, 'the honeymoon was passed in the neighbourhood to which at all times of interest in his life he turned with a strange recurring fondness . . . the quiet little village of Chalk, on the road between Gravesend and Rochester'.

The village of Chalk lies to the east of Gravesend, about a mile from the town. Some arguments have taken place about the exact house in which the honeymoon was spent. A largish house, known as the Manor House, on the corner of Thong Lane, was supposed to have that honour, as Laman Blanchard recalled how he often used to meet Dickens there, 'and here the brisk walk of Charles Dickens was always slackened, and he never failed to glance meditatively for a few moments at the windows of a corner house on the southern side of the road, advantageously situated for commanding views of the river and the far stretching landscapes beyond'. About 1905, when plans were made to mark the house with a plaque, it was discovered that the Manor House had never been let to lodgers, and could not have been the honeymoon cottage. Another candidate was found on the opposite side of the road, and the Gravesend branch of the Dickens Fellowship affixed two plaques to it in 1911. Since that day further evidence has emerged to suggest that the real cottage may have been another in the village, now demolished. It was larger than the other, with accommodation for Mrs Nash, the landlady, her family, and the Dickenses. After the birth of their first son in 1837 they returned to Chalk for a holiday, and Dickens invited his friend Thomas Beard, who had been best man at the wedding, to stay with them. A cottage consisting only of two up and two down would have been, to say the least, inadequate for the household.

Dickens loved Chalk. Always an enthusiastic walker, he would leave the lazy, already pregnant Kate (her fertility was to be one of the causes of her marital failure) and stride off alone. Said Forster: 'He would walk through the marshes to Gravesend, return by Chalk Church, and stop always to have greeting with a comical old monk who for some incomprehensible reason sits carved in stone cross-legged with a jovial pot, over the porch of that sacred edifice.' In fact, the comical old monk is not a monk at all, but a typical Romanesque gargoyle serving as the base to an empty niche. Neither Forster nor any subsequent biographer chose to allude to the figure which surmounts the niche, except as 'another grotesque': understandably, perhaps, as it is a Sheila-na-gig, one of those carvings through which Romanesque sculptors admonished, with broad enjoyment, female parishioners against the sin of Lechery, third of the Seven Deadly Sins. We are not told that Dickens greeted this unembarrassed lady 'with a friendly nod', as he did the supposed jovial monk.

About a mile from Chalk is Shorne, whose pretty little churchyard attracted Dickens so much that he conceived the idea of himself being buried, in the course of time, in 'one of the most peaceful and secluded churchyards in Kent, where wild-flowers mingle with the grass, and the soft landscape around forms the fairest spot in the garden of England'. He was writing the early chapters of *The Pickwick Papers* at the time, and weaving into it Chalk, Shorne, Gravesend and Rochester and the village of Cobham.

All his life his steps would turn towards Cobham and the Leather Bottle, the little inn where Mr Tupman, having renounced life after the loss of Rachael Wardle, was discovered by the other Pickwickians enjoying a hearty meal of 'roast fowl, bacon, ale, and etceteras, and looking as unlike a man who has taken his leave of the world as possible'.

The Leather Bottle is rather more than 'a clean and commodious ale-house' today. Coming from Gadshill by road, one arrives at the small, pretty village; on the left the old church looks down from its elevated setting towards the famous tavern, half-timbered in the manner of 1629, when it was built. The interior is like a miniature galleried inn. A little secret staircase leads to a landing from which the bedrooms open off in a row, each one bearing a familiar name on a brass plate: Pickwick, Tupman, Snodgrass, Winkle, Ben Allen, Bob Sawyer, Sam Weller. The dining-room is the very same in which Mr Tupman enjoyed his roast fowl and trimmings, and is still 'embellished with a great variety of old portraits and roughly coloured prints of some antiquity'. Rather more, indeed, than in his day: the old walls of the Leather Bottle carry something like 1,400 Dickensian prints, drawings and photographs, of Dickens himself and his scenes and characters, Mr Pickwick being the *leit-motif*. This astonishing collection is handed down from landlord to landlord: Mr Pickwick and his friends go with the inn, a rare legacy.

Dark panelling and low beams delight the lover of snugness, whether a Dickensian or not; but, if a Dickensian, the final touch of perfection is added by an inspection of an inscribed stone at

53

one corner of the building. It bears the following mysterious cypher:

X

B I L S T

U M

P S H I

S M

A R K

It was this which so enchanted the antiquarian Mr Pickwick, though, alas, its origins proved to be more recent than he had hoped, as may be gathered by copying the letters in a straight line.

The beautiful walk through Shorne Wood and Cobham Park, of which Mr Pickwick said, 'If this were the place to which all who are troubled with our friend's complaint came, I fancy their old attachment to this world would very soon return', is now approached from Chalk across a road whose turmoil would frighten even Dickens: the transmogrified Old London Road leading from the north end of the M2. It is worth the attempt to see the village and the inn where Dickens found so much enjoyment in these, his only happy days of marriage, with youth and hope still fresh upon him and fame stretching out before his feet a black and white carpet of print.

The Pickwick Papers was progressing, and a royal progress it was indeed. From the original idea of a kind of sporting comic strip it had turned into the saga of a benevolent old dilettante, Samuel Pickwick, Esquire, attended on his quest for scientific and antiquarian knowledge by his faithful followers, Winkle, lady-killing Tupman, poetical Snodgrass, and the ebullient Cockney Sam Weller. It was vibrant with a sparkling humour of a quality the world had not yet enjoyed. Dickens set this quintessence of himself as he then was in the previous decade, beginning the story in 1827. The illustrations were by Hablot K. Browne, using the pseudonym of 'Phiz' to match Dickens's pen name 'Boz'. Seymour, the original illustrator, had committed suicide, an unhappy circumstance for him but possibly a fortunate one for posterity.

Phiz's drawings riot alongside Dickens's prose, a cheerful cartoon-ist's-eye-view of the England of George IV. It is a country peopled by the children of Rowlandson's and Gillray's subjects, drawn a generation before: less gross, less brutal, less bawdy, they bear their bodies in a more seemly fashion and show considerably less of them, but they are recognizable descendants. Over-fat, over-thin, dwarfish or gigantic, they are caricatures down to the last bulge or wrinkle. The three young men, Tupman, Snodgrass and Winkle, appear by their faces to be some fifty years old, and of a quite startling unattractiveness. The young ladies have simpering faces and bedpost waists, the children are hideous imps, the dowagers leering vultures. The overall effect, however, is richly comic, and the grotesquerie of the persons is offset by the beauty of their settings, casually enough thrown at us by Phiz, ignored by Boz. Lush, open countryside, huge beamed kitchens hung with hams, roaring fires in enormous fireplaces, simple, beautiful furniture which knew not mass production, are the surroundings of the humble people in cottage and inn. Lawyers work in such chambers as Mr Serjeant Snubbin's: 'The furniture of the room was old and ricketty; the doors of the book-case were rotting on their hinges; the dust flew out from the carpet in little clouds at every step; the blinds were yellow with age and dirt.' Phiz's drawing shows an early eighteenth-century room of noble pro-portions, a moulded cornice bordering the high ceiling, the cup-boards, ornately carved, the walls handsomely panelled. Even chambers as Mr Serjeant Snubbin's: 'The furniture of the room at Bath and its surrounding apartments, he refers merely in passing to the 'handsome mirrors, chalked floors, girandoles, and wax-candles', and makes no attempt to describe that unique building. Later in the chapter he realizes that he has not done so, and gives us a facetious word-picture omitting any architectural appreciation; nor does he comment on the wonderful sweep of Royal Crescent, outside one of the doors of which Mr Winkle's embarrassing interlude with Mrs Dowler and the sedan-chair took place. Yet, between him and his illustrator, a microcosm of that vanished England of the 1820s is created; not exactly accurate, very far from serious, frequently grotesque to a degree, yet wholly delight-ful as a representational account could never be.

The Pickwickians very naturally followed the route of the honey-mooning Dickenses from the Golden Cross in London to Kent, along the old Roman Road which is now the A2 and which, since it has been bypassed by the M2, retains many of the buildings which saw the 'Commodore' coach rattle by. Dickens takes the Pickwickians straight to Rochester; from the beautiful bridge (long demolished and replaced by an extremely unbeautiful one) the travellers admire the shell of the castle. 'Magnificent ruin!' says Mr Snodgrass, with poetic fervour, while the actor Jingle apostrophizes it in his customary staccato style: 'Ah! fine place . . . glorious pile—frowning walls—tottering arches—dark nooks—crumbling staircases—old Cathedral, too—earthy smell—pilgrims' feet worn away the old steps—little Saxon doors—confessionals like money-takers' boxes at theatres.' Even this facetious view of Rochester's antiquities reflects Dickens's obsession with the macabre: 'sarcophagus—fine place—old legends too—strange stories—capital.' When he was a dying man, once again describing Rochester, this element of death and decay would predominate.

The travellers proceeded to the Bull inn—'good house—nice beds'. In *Sketches by Boz* Dickens calls it 'a large [house] with red brick and stone front. A pretty spacious hall, ornamented with evergreen plants, terminates in a perspective view of the bar, and a glass case, in which are displayed a choice variety of delicacies ready for dressing . . . opposite doors lead to the "Coffee" and "Commercial" rooms; and a great, wide, rambling staircase . . . conducts to galleries of bedrooms, and labyrinths of sitting-rooms'.

The red-brick and stone front of the Bull would be recognizable to Dickens (though the inn has been renamed the Royal Victoria and Bull, in commemoration of a visit from Victoria in 1836). The fine pillared entrance to the inn-yard suggests something nobler than a car-park beyond. But, once through it, the traveller perceives that great changes have come to the Bull. A bewildering assortment of bars and restaurants invite; one bar has a painstaking late Victorian décor, and bears the name of Great Expectations. The original hall has been kept, but is rather smaller than the 'pretty spacious' description that Dickens gave it, and the staircase is hardly great, wide, or rambling, though it does lead (as in Phiz's illustration) to the ballroom. This has kept its proportions and a general resemblance to the 'long room, with crimson-covered benches, and wax candles in glass chandeliers' in which Mr Jingle cut out Dr Slammer with the wealthy widow, and the aristocracy of the dockyard preserved their dignity. But with the modernization of the Bull the charm has gone; the old house tries too strenuously to be a modern hotel, with the effect (to use an appropriately Pickwickian metaphor) that might be produced by Mr Wardle's mother attempting to pass herself off as Arabella Allen.

The rest of Rochester High Street—all, with its immediate environs, that is left of the ancient town—belongs to later books. We now follow the Pickwickians to Dingley Dell, home of the hospitable squire Wardle, and scene of so many festivities. Much argument has taken place about its exact location. The nearby town of 'Muggleton' may have been Maidstone, or it may have been West Malling. Maidstone seems to fit in with Dickens's description of Dingley Dell as being fifteen miles from Rochester, and not above two miles from Muggleton: that is if Cob Tree Hall, Sandling, to the north of Maidstone, was the original of Manor Farm, Dingley Dell. Mr William Spong, who lived at Cob Tree Hall and died there in November 1839, is thought by some to have been the prototype of Wardle. Cob Tree has just the sort of pond on which Mr Pickwick's accident might have taken place that icy Christmas, and old residents even remembered a rookery in its trees, towards the inhabitants of which Mr Winkle's uncertain gun was pointed, only to find its target in the left arm of his unfortunate friend Tupman. At Cob Tree, too, is a great kitchen exactly suited to the Christmas Eve revels so zestfully described by Boz and drawn by Phiz (though he calls it 'the best sitting-room').*

From Dickens's home territory the Pickwickians moved out on the trail of his journeys as a reporter in 1834, to the part of England which, after Kent, he knew best. Here the localities are neither so specifically identified nor so affectionately described. Eatanswill, that 'rotten borough', may have been Eaton Socon, but was more probably Sudbury. Bury St Edmunds retains its own name. The idyllic journey there, through the August fields where sunburnt gleaners pause 'to gaze upon the passengers with curious eyes', may still be recaptured in the quiet lanes of Suffolk, where the twentieth century seems not yet born. Endless unpainted canvases of Constable and Crome unroll, pastoral scenes of meadow and hamlet, mill and church, living and yet with a kind of arrested life, as Dickens saw them. 'You cast a look behind you, as you

---

* A pleasant and ingenious reconstruction of such a kitchen exists in the basement of Dickens House, 48 Doughty Street.

turn the corner of the road. The women and children have resumed their labour, the reaper once more stoops to his work, the cart-horses have moved on, and all are again in motion.'

Bury St Edmunds, 'a handsome little town of thriving and cleanly appearance', is bigger and busier than it was, but still pleasant. Mr Pickwick's coach pulled up at the 'large inn, situated in a wide, open street, nearly facing the old abbey'. The Angel still stands on Angel Hill, in Market Square, the town's principal inn, and is proud of its place in fiction: 'assoc. Pickwick', proclaims its entry in the R.A.C. book. Here, in the stable-yard, Sam Weller encountered the mulberry-liveried Job Trotter and innocently made Mr Pickwick once more the victim of the devious Jingle; from this establishment Sam and his master set out on the campaign which ended so embarrassingly at a boarding-school for young ladies. The school building, called in the book Westgate House, has been tentatively identified as Southgate House in Southgate Street. But Dickens may well have been thinking of Eastgate House in Rochester, which he used in *Edwin Drood* as a girls' school.

Yet another misfortune overtook Mr Pickwick at Ipswich. For a middle-aged single gentleman of modest disposition to find himself by accident sharing a bedroom with a spinster lady was a truly horrifying experience; the more so because at the moment of realization he was semi-clothed and had donned that highly suggestive article, a nightcap, and she, in preparation for bed, was wearing curl-papers and brushing her back hair. 'The very idea of exhibiting his nightcap to a lady overpowered him, but he had tied those confounded strings in a knot, and do what he would he couldn't get it off.' How had such a situation come to pass? Very simply. The rambling geography of the inn had confused Mr Pickwick's normally alert mind so greatly that after exploring passage after passage, peeping into room after room, he had entered the wrong bedchamber.

The Great White Horse at Ipswich remains unchanged apart from necessary modernization. Dickens would have approved of this, for he entirely failed to appreciate the Horse as it was when he saw it when reporting for the *Suffolk Chronicle* in 1835. The exterior, he said, was 'rendered the more conspicuous by a stone statue of some rampacious animal with a flowing mane and tail, distantly resembling an insane cart-horse, which is elevated above the principal door. The Great White Horse is famous in the neighbourhood, in the same degree as a prize ox, or county-paper-chronicled turnip, or unwieldy pig—for its enormous size. Never were such labyrinths of uncarpeted passages, such clusters of mouldy, ill-lighted rooms, such huge numbers of small dens for eating or sleeping in, beneath any one roof'. He proceeded further to castigate the Horse's menu—'a bit of fish and a steak were served up to the travellers' after an hour's wait—very poor, on both counts, by the standards of the time, particularly when washed down by 'a bottle of the worst possible port wine'.

There is a note of personal resentment in the description, supported by a statement made in 1899, when the *Suffolk Chronicle* had merged with two other papers, that Dickens, when staying at the inn in 1835, had got into some such situation as Mr Pickwick's, and as a result had developed a strong prejudice against the house. No evidence of this, or of any other cause, appears in his correspondence, but dislike the Great White Horse he certainly did. Perhaps the very poor fish and steak were responsible.

The same rampacious animal high-steps today (he is a perfectly ordinary fellow, sturdily handsome, and without a gleam of insanity in his eye) over the pillared portico. The ancient inn-yard, round which the galleries once extended, has been glassed over. Carpets are beneath one's feet instead of cobbles and, in the space where stable-boys, Bootses and servants had clattered and whistled, one may take tea or coffee or something stronger, meet friends or pay one's bill. Dickens's 'clusters of mouldy, ill-lighted rooms' and 'small dens for eating or sleeping in' are, in fact, a delightful warren of old rooms blessedly unchanged in shape and size, for the most part. 'Mr Pickwick's Room' is preserved, with four-posters resembling those of Phiz's illustration. To see the Great White Horse is to see what the galleried inns of London were like, the White Hart, the Tabard, all the others which have been swept away. The fact that the Horse did not follow them is due to the magnificent efforts, against heavy odds, of the Dickens Fellowship, among other gallant defenders of that splendid inn.

Some inns immortalized by the Pickwickian pilgrimage have retained their names and situations but lost their forms and identities. The White Horse Cellar in Piccadilly would be unrecognizable to them today, particularly if they approached it, as one may, from that other cellar, the underground station. The

Belle Sauvage, Tony Weller's headquarters, long demolished, stood by Ludgate Circus. The Magpie and Stump was probably a composite portrait, the name taken from a vanished inn in Clare Market and the building from the George IV in Portsmouth Street. There is a Magpie and Stump today opposite the Old Bailey. The George and Vulture, where Mr Pickwick was 'at present suspended', is also happily still with us, in George Yard, Lombard Street, a lonely survivor of those City chop-houses in which gentlemen could eat steak and drink porter in the snug seclusion of a bunker, the high wooden back of which secured them from that curse of modern eating-out, other people's conversation. It is difficult to find, even when you have got into Lombard Street; you must go through Change Alley and Birchin Lane to track it down where it huddles in narrow Castle Court, as though it were afraid that, when you do find it, you may pull it down. The Horn Tavern in Knightrider Street, off Ludgate Hill, remains much as it was when the imprisoned Mr Pickwick ordered from it a select dinner for his friends.

Those hostelries which received the Pickwickians and their creator in the West Country have not all disappeared, though the Bush at Bristol went in 1864 and the White Hart in Bath, opposite the Pump Room, was replaced in 1867 by the Grand Pump Room Hotel. It was owned in Dickens's time by a Mr Moses Pickwick. The inn where the footmen of Bath met together to enjoy themselves, and where Sam Weller partook of the 'friendly swarry, consisting of a boiled leg of mutton with the usual trimmings', was the Beaufort Arms, just off Queen Square. Dickens, for some reason, called it a greengrocer's shop. The strange old inn, with its even stranger old chair, where Tom Smart the Bagman had his curious adventure, may have been the Waggon and Horses at Beckhampton, on the Marlborough Downs. The Hop Pole at Tewkesbury, where the party stopped to dine on their last pilgrimage, survives. At Towcester, the Pomfret Arms still offers refreshment to the traveller, and remembers that it was once the Saracen's Head, recommended to his master by Sam. 'There's beds here, sir . . . everything clean and comfortable. Wery good little dinner, sir.'

The last inn of all, 'Osborne's in the Adelphi', where the amorous difficulties of Emily Wardle and Mr Snodgrass were finally straightened out, went in 1936 when the lovely, historic Adelphi

60

Terrace was destroyed and replaced by characterless buildings resembling nothing so much as giant cinemas. At 'Osborne's' (in reality the Adelphi Hotel) Gibbon had stayed when he returned from Lausanne with the final volumes of *The Decline and Fall of the Roman Empire*. Isaac d'Israeli was resident there soon after the wedding which resulted in his glorious son Benjamin. Thomas Rowlandson died there, his last caricature completed. Three years earlier, the poor 'Queen of the Cannibal Islands', wife of King Kamahame, there succumbed to measles. But none of these memories remain to haunt the site of the corner of Adam Street and John Street. 'Osborne's' survives only as the place where a fictional evening was excellently spent. 'Arabella was very charming, Mr Wardle very jovial, Mr Pickwick very harmonious, Mr Ben Allen very uproarious, the lovers very silent, Mr Winkle very talkative, and all of them very happy.'

6

Family Life and Authorship

If you go to Doughty Street, Bloomsbury, today, your entry will not be barred from the John Street end by 'a porter in a gold-laced hat with the Doughty arms on the buttons of his mulberry-coloured coat to prevent anyone except with a mission to one of the houses ever intruding on the exclusive territory'. The porter and his lodge have gone, together with his opposite number and *his* lodge at the Guilford Street end, and the Foundling Hospital, just beyond. But Doughty Street is still, as Dickens's friend Edmund Yates described it, 'a broad wholesome street', wide and airy, with handsome unspoiled Georgian houses. Into one of them, No. 48, Dickens, Kate and baby Charley moved during the last weekend of March 1837, amid 'worry and turmoil'.

Rescued from demolition in 1922 by the Dickens Fellowship, the house became a permanent memorial to Dickens, with a library and a matchless collection of Dickensian pictures and relics. In its own right it is a fine house, typical of its time, with a peaceful atmosphere; more peaceful than might be expected after the storm and sunshine of the mercurial young man's residence in it. His face is everywhere on its walls, sometimes youthful, with, as Forster said, 'the eager, restless, energetic outlook on each several feature, that seemed to tell so little of a student or writer of books, and so much of a man of action and business in the world. Light and motion flashed from every part of it. "It was as if made of steel" was said of it . . . by a most original and delicate observer, the late Mrs Carlyle'. That ardent, vivacious face has been captured perfectly by the artist-friends whom it fascinated; to see these portraits is to know the young Dickens. The man he became is less immediately attractive; in the lined, bearded face of the famous novelist there is secrecy, sorrow, a kind of defiance, for he no longer knows himself.

Kate, plump in young matronhood, is far prettier than her younger sister Mary, judging from Phiz's portrait of the sixteen-year-old girl who came to Doughty Street with them. But Dickens thought the drawing worthless as 'a record of that dear face'. In 1837, after only one year, he was already subconsciously dissatisfied with his marriage; sufficiently so to transfer to Mary his high ideal of womanhood. Sexually inaccessible, as his sister-in-law, she provided him with the outlet for romantic ardour which the all too accessible Kate could not provide. Mary was 'the grace and life of our home', 'young, beautiful and good'.

A mere month after the Dickenses had moved into Doughty Street—Saturday, 6th May—that grace and life ended. They had all been to the theatre and, on returning, after cheerful good nights, Charles and Kate retired to their bedroom on the second floor, Mary to hers next to it. Soon after going to bed she became suddenly ill, and died the following afternoon in her brother-in-law's arms, probably from something like an aortic aneurism. Dickens wrote to a friend the next day: 'She has been to us what we can never replace, and has left a blank which no one who ever knew her can have the faintest hope of seeing supplied.' The sentence was prophetic. Death had taken from him, with shocking violence, something which he desperately needed, which never would be replaced. Her image—her ghost, he believed—followed him all the days of his life. He searched for her in other women, but never found her again.

He could not work. Suspending the further publication of *The Pickwick Papers* for one month, he moved out to Hampstead, to try the effect of 'quiet and change' on his shocked nerves. The country retreat was Collins's Farm, on the western edge of Hampstead Heath, behind the Bull and Bush. Now known as Wylde's, it stands there still, a private house, rural and pleasant as when it provided a haven for Dickens and poor Kate (who had a miscarriage after the tragedy): 'a cottage of our own, with large gardens, and everything on a small but comfortable scale.'

When the present authors were allowed to look over Wylde's, by the kindness of its owner, Mr P. D. R. Venning, it was being thoroughly and intelligently restored. Last century it became the headquarters of the Fabian Society and then a kind of hostel for students. It is a large cottage, partly Elizabethan, beamed and ingle-nooked; as rural as any lodging Dickens would have found in Kent. The beautiful woodland ride in which it is set is a match for it, a patch of country within a stone's throw of Golders Green.

From Collins's Dickens and Kate must have walked, when Kate was well enough, through the woods to Jack Straw's Castle, up the hill, looking across the heath. A modest, four-square house, with no other ornament than its slender-pillared porch and broad, bottle-glassed bow windows on either side, it was one of Dickens's favourite haunts all his life: that 'good 'ous, where we can have a red-hot chop for dinner, and a glass of good wine' to which he introduced Forster. It appears only once in the novels, when David Copperfield, after a bad night, walks to Hampstead and has breakfast 'on the Heath', returning 'along the watered roads and through a pleasant smell of summer flowers'. For half a century and more after his death it was a bourne for Dickensian pilgrims, who were shown the bedroom he slept in (a doubtful attribution) and the chair he sat in. A few years ago Jack Straw's was demolished, on the excuse that too little of the original structure remained to be of interest, and was replaced by a curious fortress-like building. But there are still gardens to drink in, on a summer evening, as he would have done in that sad summer of 1837.

The Spaniards Inn, east of Jack Straw's along the country lane leading to Highgate, was another of Dickens's ports of call. Unlike its neighbour tavern, it has survived not only the demolishers but also the 'improvers' of ancient buildings. When last seen, its panelled parlour, 'snug' and hall were much as they had been, though Dickens would not recognize the bar. The gardens have remained as pleasant as when they drew Londoners by the score up the hill to take tea, as Mrs Bardell and her friends did on the day of her arrest. It was a somewhat different journey from today's swift underground trip to Hampstead or Golders Green tube stations, thence by the little 210 bus to the door. Travelling by stage-coach, it took the Bardell party two hours from Goswell Street, which runs southward from the Angel, Islington (it is now Goswell Road), to reach the Spaniards. In spite of the absence in those days of licensing laws, the ladies and their escort Mr Raddle drank tea and consumed bread-and-butter for seven. Mr Raddle got into serious trouble for not having confined himself to ordering tea for six, for 'what could have been easier than for Tommy to have drank out of anybody's cup—or everybody's, if that was all—when the waiter wasn't looking?' Perhaps it is not altogether surprising that their refreshments were, by the standards of their day, meagre: at Goswell Street they had already refreshed themselves with 'sundry plates of oranges and biscuits, and a bottle of old crusted port—that at one and nine—with another of the celebrated East India sherry at fourteenpence'.

Mrs Rogers's reflection 'How sweet the country is, to be sure!' would not be entirely applicable to the surroundings of the Spaniards a century and a half later. Behind it stretches the tidy world of Hampstead Garden Suburb, built on what was wild common land. Golders Green, then reached by a dark, lonely lane dangerous for nocturnal foot-passengers, is a maelstrom of shops and traffic and Hampstead itself has grown out of all proportion. But the heath still lies open and lovely, green fields and hawthorn bushes and great oaks which saw Dickens striding past. You may still walk through the woods to the west, down to 'Collins's Farm'. And in the garden of the Spaniards Londoners bask and chatter and ponder on the small gravestones of the departed dogs belonging to the inn. Blackbirds, glutted with cherries, rest on the high wall.

Soon Dickens was back to Bloomsbury and work. In the autumn of 1836 he had had an offer to edit a new magazine, *Bentley's Miscellany*. In this appeared his next novel, in the usual monthly parts. It was *Oliver Twist*, the tale of a poor child born in a workhouse, entrapped at the age of nine in London's criminal underworld: a natural subject for the young man who had become so indignant when reporting parliamentary debates about the laws affecting the conditions of the poor. The new book did not take London readers very far from home. Oliver's workhouse is impossible to identify. It was seventy-five or eighty miles north of London, on a stage-coach route which entered the City through Barnet. Oliver arrived at Barnet after a gruelling walk lasting seven days. The little Hertfordshire town is not greatly changed, in spite of its growth. It would not be quite true to say, as Dickens did, that 'every other house in Barnet was a tavern, large or small',

65

but quite a number of taverns remain, including a grandiose descendant of the Red Lion, to which, in March 1838, Dickens rode with John Forster to dine (and, incidentally, to get away from home where Kate had just given birth to their second child, Mary, or Mamie). The Artful Dodger led Oliver into London by way of a countrified route which is now Archway Road and Holloway Road, towards the bourne of Saffron Hill and the house near Field Lane where, in a room whose walls and ceiling were 'perfectly black with age and dirt', lurked the thief-master Fagin.

The Fagin district is much altered, and for the better. Saffron Hill, which runs parallel with Farringdon Road from Clerkenwell Road, is strictly respectable and commercial. The Three Cripples, that low public-house frequented by Bill Sikes and his cronies, has never been identified. It is not inviting, with its glaring gas-lights, pall of tobacco smoke, jingling piano and unsavoury customers, but the reality would have been a good deal less inviting. Dickens knew such places well. Living only just across Gray's Inn Lane, he could stroll at night round such dark and dangerous districts as Field Lane, fascinated by the horrors of which he could give his public only an edited version. Public executions still took place in front of Newgate; not for mere playfulness did Sikes terrify Fagin by miming the tying of a knot under the left ear, and the sideways fall of the head. Sikes and Monks are melodramatic villains, using the language of the contemporary theatre; their actual speech would have been quite unprintable, as shocking to Dickens's readers as a literal description of the drunkenness of the clients of the Three Cripples. Not for nothing did the young Queen Victoria's government, within the first two years of her reign, bring in the Metropolitan Police Act, which ordained that all public houses within fifteen miles of Charing Cross must shut on Sundays until one o'clock, and that publicans must not sell drink to young persons under sixteen years of age. By 1839 the days were gone when a small Charles Dickens could have treated himself to a beer in the Red Lion, Parliament Street. In 1837 it was still possible for a child to drink, and to see its parents drinking, the notorious Blue Ruin: cheap doctored gin which in the gaudy new gin palaces helped its drinkers to forget the misery of their lives and, eventually, turned them literally blue, 'a ghostly corpse-like kind of blue, which made one shudder'. London was bigger, uglier, poorer than when Hogarth had painted *Gin Lane* as a horrible warning. Tennyson, singer of May Queens and Maud, noticed that the Glad New Year in London's dram shops was not prettily celebrated:

And the vitriol madness flushes up in the ruffian's brain,
Till the filthy by-lane rings to the yell of the trampled wife,
And chalk and alum and plaster are sold to the poor for bread,
And the spirit of murder works in the very means of life.

Oliver Twist, though it could not right all such wrongs, did much for the condition of children more under-privileged than we in our Welfare State can possibly imagine. Poor Oliver was the cats'-paw of the thieves, small enough to be put through a pantry window to let them into the house. They took him down to Chertsey, pausing at the Coach and Horses, Isleworth, before continuing to their destination, the house of Mrs Maylie. Where was this 'detached house surrounded by a wall', about a quarter of a mile from Chertsey village? Percy Fitzgerald, warm friend, disciple and indefatigable chronicler of Dickens, has identified it as Pycroft House, just under St Anne's Hill, a Queen Anne building with 'an abundance of little offices and outhouses', in one of which 'Oliver's window' used to be pointed out. It is now part of the Sir William Perkins School.

The many changes which have overtaken London Bridge had, until recently, left more or less alone the steps on its Surrey side where Nancy promised to walk 'every Sunday night from eleven until the clock strikes twelve . . . if I am alive', and where she was overheard by Noah Claypole talking to Mr Brownlow and Rose Maylie—a conversation which led to her dreadful death. The recesses, in one of which Noah hid that night, disappeared however when the bridge was widened in 1901, and the steps themselves fell victim to the 1969 bridge rebuilding. After the murder, Sikes in his headlong flight went northwards along a road Dickens knew well: Islington, Highgate, Ken Wood, the Vale of Health, a detour to Hendon and then an uneasy return to the heath where he could hide and see any pursuers. Then, at last, 'he got away, and shaped his course for Hatfield'.

The tavern into which he and his poor limping dog crept was the Eight Bells, at the foot of Fore Street, leading up to the Old Palace and Hatfield House. When last visited this tiny inn was the most unspoiled of all those mentioned in the novels and still identifiable. Dark-panelled, wainscotted, low-ceilinged, it crouches at the foot of the steep cobbled street just as when the scanty light from its windows guided Sikes to it. In this tap-room (presumably the main bar) he sat 'in the furthest corner, and ate and drank alone, or rather with his dog', until the wandering pedlar's jocose offer of a composition which would remove bloodstains drove him 'with a hideous imprecation' from the place. Dickens has juggled with geography in making the great fire at which Sikes assisted some distance from Hatfield; it was, of course, at Hatfield House itself.*

Hatfield reappears in the story 'Mrs Lirriper's Lodgings' (*Christmas Stories*): Mr Lirriper elected to be buried there, 'not that it was his native place but that he had a liking for the Salisbury Arms where we went upon our wedding-day and passed as happy a fortnight as ever happy was'; and Mrs Lirriper, after paying his debts, 'put a sandwich and a drop of sherry in a little basket and went down to Hatfield churchyard outside the coach and kissed my hand and laid it with a kind of proud and swelling love on my husband's grave'. The little churchyard, the church where the Cecils lie, the graceful remnant of Archbishop Morton's building and the noble house itself are all as she would see them, though somewhat cleaner, and with the additional attraction of tea in the Old Palace.

From this idyllic setting Sikes fled back to London to die, symbolically, from hanging as he attempted to escape over the rooftops of one of the desolate houses on Jacob's Island, 'the filthiest, the strangest, the most extraordinary of the many localities that are hidden in London, wholly unknown, even by name, to the great mass of its inhabitants'. In Dickens's own time a London alderman—an amazing alderman, said Dickens—'publicly declared that Jacob's Island did not exist, and never had existed'. A riverside slum of a kind no longer to be found in this country, it was slowly improved away throughout the nineteenth century. Its site was about a mile eastward of London Bridge, a quarter of a mile or so from Tower Bridge. Gone, too, is old Newgate Prison and the condemned cell where Fagin begged for mercy. But there is a sporting chance that Mr Brownlow's house in Craven Street, Strand, has survived the building of Charing Cross Railway.

* See page 51.

10

The Great White Horse, Ipswich, where Dickens stayed in 1835, and where Mr Pickwick's adventure involving the middle-aged lady in curl-papers took place.

George and Vulture Inn, Castle Court, City of London, the headquarters of Mr Pickwick after he left Mrs Bardell's.

48 Doughty Street, Bloomsbury, Dickens's home, 1837–9, the period in ▷ which he soared to fame. It is now the headquarters of the Dickens Fellowship and the principal Dickensian museum.

Wylde's Farm, formerly Collins's Farm, Hampstead, where Dickens went to recover from the shock of Mary Hogarth's death.

'Dotheboys Hall', Bowes, as it appeared in about 1838, the year of Nicholas Nickleby. *Drawing by E. Ridsdale Tate.*

13

14

The Spaniards Inn,
Hampstead. It was well
known to Dickens and
its gardens were the
scene of Mrs Bardell's
ill-fated tea-party in
The Pickwick Papers.

The Bedford Hotel,
Brighton, where Dickens
stayed in 1848, and
where Mr Dombey
lodged when visiting
Paul.

15

16

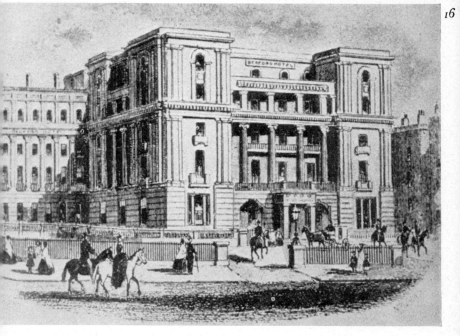

18

Dickens House, Broadstairs, Kent. In David Copperfield *Dickens places it in Dover, as the home of Betsey Trotwood.*

◁ *Bleak House, Broadstairs, Kent, the family's holiday home for many years. Then named Fort House, it has no connection with the novel.*

19

Tong Church as Cattermole saw it:
'a very aged, ghostly place'.
Illustration to The Old Curiosity
Shop.

The Little Midshipman in Dombey
and Son, *the shop sign of Solomon*
Gills. Actually the sign of a nautical
instrument-maker in the City, and
a familiar sight to Dickens, it is
preserved in 48 Doughty Street,
headquarters of the Dickens
Fellowship.   20

With 48 Doughty Street full of an ailing wife, crying babies and their attendants, it must have been something of a relief to Dickens to dash up to Yorkshire in search of material for *Nicholas Nickleby*. Still tilting against the monsters who oppressed helpless children, he was out to denounce in print the notorious Yorkshire boarding-schools to which unwanted, often illegitimate, boys were sent out of their guardians' way. A cold coach journey took him and his illustrator, Hablot K. Browne, up to Grantham in January 1838. There he found 'the very best inn I have ever put up at', and sent his fictitious travellers there as well. 'One of the best inns in England, the George' is still three-starred. The Old George and New Inn at Greta Bridge, their next halt, was 'a house standing alone in the midst of a dreary moor'.* But he found entertainment there, and pressed on to Barnard Castle, a market-town high above the River Tees, over the border in County Durham. There he and Browne stayed at the King's Head, in the market-place, and again were favourably impressed by northern hospitality. Whether he stayed for two days at the King's Head, or transferred himself to the Unicorn at Bowes, is a matter of conjecture. Many people swore until their dying day that he stayed in the district for a full six weeks: actually his stay was for only two days.

He made preliminary inquiries about schools at Startforth, near by, but it seemed that the village of Bowes held his real quarry, a man named Shaw whom he was to transmute into the sadistic Squeers; whether rightly or wrongly will never be known, for Shaw was considered worthy of a stained-glass window in the church after his death, and was generally said to be 'one of the least bad' of the Yorkshire schoolmasters. Be that as it may, both Squeers and Shaw had one eye, and it seems likely that Dickens wanted to identify his model clearly by this characteristic. In the case of Shaw there are facts, as well as traditions. He had been tried in 1823 for cruelty to his pupils, one of the pupils giving horrifying evidence: 'We had no supper. We had warm water and milk for tea and dry bread. We had hay and straw beds, and one sheet to each bed, in which four or five boys slept; there were about thirty beds in one room, and a large tub in the middle . . . we had fleas every other morning . . . I mean we had quills furnished us to flea the beds every other morning, and we caught a good beating

* Probably the original of the Holly-Tree Inn of *Christmas Stories*.

if we did not fill the quills with fleas. We had the skimmings of the pot every Sunday afternoon, the usher offered a penny for every maggot, and the boys found more than a quart full, but he did not give them the money. . . . On one occasion (in October) I felt a weakness in my eyes, and could not write my copy. The defendant [Shaw] said he would beat me. On the next day I could not see at all, and I told Mr Shaw, who sent me, with three others, to the wash-house. He always sent those boys who were ill to the wash-house, as he had no doctor. Those who were totally blind were sent into a room. . . . I was in the room two months, and the doctor then discharged me, saying I had lost one eye. In fact I was blind with both.' Some of the letters and exercise-books of Shaw's pupils can be seen at Dickens House.

Local good opinions of Shaw (and the locals no doubt made a fair livelihood out of the presence of the school in their midst) cannot counterbalance the fact that such brutalities and deprivations did go on at 'Dotheboys Hall', as Dickens called Shaw-Squeers's establishment. If anything, he softened some details and withheld others too horrible to mention to his public.

The Hall itself, 'a long, cold-looking house, with a few straggling out-buildings behind', stands at the western end of the one-street village of Bowes. In 1899 two Dickensians, H. Snowden Ward and Catherine Ward, went to photograph the exterior and were told by their driver, who had been through the house a few weeks before, when it was being auctioned, that 'the garret room, without light and without ventilation, had its ceiling (once white-washed) covered with candle-smoked names and initials, as far as could be reached by boys standing on their beds; and although he was not a man educated to luxury, the sight of that sleeping-room justified, to his mind, all that was written in *Nickleby*'.

Today Dotheboys Hall has changed its function and ambience utterly: it is a café. The long, low grey stone house of two storeys which the Wards saw was converted by later tenants into a sort of suburban villa (it still bears the name The Villa). The classroom and dormitories had been demolished before this, but perhaps they felt that they would be more comfortable in a house which in no way resembled what it had been, and would thus be rid of the ghosts of flea-ridden, starved, blinded boys. No unhappier ghosts, surely, could walk anywhere.

It has been worked out that there were usually more than eight hundred boys being 'educated' in the neighbourhood of Bowes at one time, at Shaw's school, Bowes Hall, and Startforth Hall. How many of them died is impossible to tell; some lie in unrecorded graves. But two stones, in the south-east corner of Bowes Church-yard, tell of two who 'unfortunately died'. One reads:

Here lie

the Remains of

George Ashton Taylor

Son of John Taylor

of Trowbridge Wilts

who died suddenly at

Mr William Shaw's Academy

of this place April 13th 1822

aged 19 years.

Young reader thou must die

But after this the judgement.

Dickens saw it, and wrote to Mrs S. C. Hall in December 1838: 'I think his ghost put Smike into my mind, upon the spot.' After this the judgment, indeed.

He was too concerned with his crusade, and too cold, to concern himself with much sight-seeing on this northern excursion; but at York (staying at the Black Swan, Coney Street) he did attend service in the Minster, and made its Five Sisters window the subject of a traveller's tale in *Nicholas Nickleby*, perhaps because he could thus express, in the medieval legend of a beloved young sister dead in youth, the extent of his continuing grief for Mary Hogarth. A suggestion for a very different story may have come to him at Barnard Castle. It was said that on the opposite side of the street from the hotel was a shop with a large clock-face for a sign, and the name Humphrey surrounding it. Mr Humphrey him-self was sure that this suggested to Dickens the title *Master Humphrey's Clock* for the series of stories which provided links between his next two novels, *The Old Curiosity Shop* and *Barnaby Rudge*.

Having fulfilled his serious intention, Dickens abandoned himself to enjoyment in the remainder of *Nicholas Nickleby*. One of the most zestful, continuously amusing of the novels, it seems to belong in period more to the Regency than to the year in which it was written, 1838. Echoing the picaresque romances he had loved as a boy, *Peregrine Pickle*, *Roderick Random* and their like, it carried his young hero Nicholas from one lively scene to another. Most of the London of *Nicholas Nickleby* is the West End, not the dark City of *Oliver Twist*. Much of that London was Georgian and is no more to be seen. In Golden Square, behind Piccadilly Circus (which did not then exist), Ralph Nickleby's house may be one of those that are left, put to commercial uses. The Saracen's Head on Snow Hill, from which Squeers and his party set off for Yorkshire, has its memorial only in Dickens's fancifully funny comparison with what Snow Hill should be: 'the name is such a good one!' The house in Thames Street, by a wharf, in which Ralph lodged his sister-in-law and niece, must have fallen to pieces long ago; it was 'old and gloomy, and black . . . sullen and dark were the rooms . . . an empty dog-kennel, some bones of animals, fragments of iron hoops, and staves of old casks, lay strewn about, but no life was stirring there. It was a picture of cold, silent decay'. 'This house depresses and chills one,' remarked Kate Nickleby, understandably. It was just the sort of house Dickens most disliked, and he used it with unconscious symbolism as the 'tomb' to which Ralph, the Wicked Uncle, wished to condemn his unwanted dependants.

It was not only unsavoury, but about as inconvenient a site as Ralph could have devised for his young niece's home. Every morning, at a quarter to eight, she had to walk to her work at Madame Mantalini's millinery and dress-making establishment in Wigmore Street, near Cavendish Square. If Dickens was really thinking of Thames Street as the site of the decayed mansion, the journey he gave poor Kate is almost incredible. We are told that the Nicklebys' first progress to it from Miss La Creevy's in the Strand was 'a long and slow drive' by coach. Well it might be, for Thames Street extends from the present Blackfriars Station to Tower Hill. We do not hear at which end of the street Ralph's house stood, but, assuming it to be at the eastern end, Kate would have had to make her way by a maze of small streets into Fleet Street, up Chancery Lane into Holborn (this would have been a more likely route for an unaccompanied young female than the sleazy district now covered by Aldwych and Kingsway), through Bloomsbury to the Oxford Road, now Oxford Street, and thence up Regent Street to Cavendish Square. She was a country girl who had not been in London long and would be unlikely to have the Londoner's knowledge of, or instinct for, short cuts. The coach route lay through streets 'crowded . . . with vehicles of every kind' to cross which would be a slow and terrifying business for a nervous provincial. Madame Mantalini's working hours were from nine in the morning until nine at night, and Kate left Thames Street at a quarter to eight. How she survived such a journey, twice daily, based as it was on her creator's passion for long walks and his indefatigable energy, is difficult to imagine, as is her bill for shoe repairs.

The original houses of Cavendish Square which survive give a fair idea of Madame Mantalini's house and showrooms, the shop below which was let off to an importer of otto of roses. Cadogan Place, where lived Mrs Wititterly, Kate's next employer, has resisted demolition and improvement, but since the steep social rise of Belgravia can hardly be said any more to 'look down upon Sloane Street' or even to 'think Brompton low'. A startling change, however, has come over the face of the street in which lodged Newman Noggs and the Kenwigs family. Dickens's description is worth quoting: 'In that quarter of London in which Golden Square is situated, there is a bygone, faded, tumble-down street, with two irregular rows of tall meagre houses, which seem to have stared each other out of countenance years ago. The very chimneys appear to have grown dismal and melancholy, from having had nothing better to look at than the chimneys over the way. . . . The fowls who peck about the kennels, jerking their bodies hither and thither with a gait which none but town fowls are ever seen to adopt, and which any country cock or hen would be puzzled to understand, are perfectly in keeping with the crazy habitations of their owners. Dingy, ill-plumed, drowsy flutterers, sent, like many of the neighbouring children, to get a livelihood in the streets, they . . . can scarcely raise a crow among them.'

The houses, he says, had seen better days, but were let off in rooms and floors, 'and every door has almost as many plates or bell-handles as there are apartments within. The windows are, for the same reason, sufficiently diversified in appearance, being ornamented with every variety of common blind and curtain that can easily be imagined; while every doorway is blocked up, and rendered nearly impassable, by a motley collection of children and porter pots of all sizes, from the baby in arms and the half-pint pot, to the full-grown girl and half-gallon can'.

From this description it is difficult to recognize Carnaby Street. It is equally difficult to assess Dickens's probable reaction to its appearance today, could he return to find the very same ancient houses, the very same chimneys, but in every other respect a transformation scene more complete and amazing than any in a Drury Lane pantomime. The chimneys now have a great deal more to look at than their opposite numbers; seldom can any chimneys, anywhere, have gazed continuously upon such fantastic sights. The poor town fowls have long since pecked their way to oblivion, and have been replaced by 'birds' neither dingy nor ill-plumed. The windows, certainly, are 'diversified in appearance', but the common blinds and curtains have given way to a dazzling display of velvets, satins, leather and feathers, mock-jewels and foaming frills of nylon. The old doorways are 'rendered nearly impassable' by strange, unisex figures moving like a human river of colour, and instead of the clatter of the pint pot there is heard the implacable, resistless beat of recorded 'pop'. Dickens would fail to understand the implications of much that he would see and would be shocked by some aspects he could not fail to understand. But it is more than probable that he, who nicknamed himself The Sparkler and The Gas Light Boy, who loved floral waistcoats and flashing tiepins and stage disguise, who could not exist for long without the restless bustle of the London streets, and who revelled in human strangeness, even grotesquerie—it is more than probable that he would like Carnaby Street very much.

There are many London localities mentioned in *Nicholas Nickleby*, from Lawrence Pountney Hill, where the Cheeryble Brothers lived, to the Brays' lodging in the Rules of the King's Bench, off Westminster Bridge Road, but few are readily identifiable now. It has been conjectured that the handsome hotel where Nicholas accidentally heard his sister's name bandied about in masculine conversation was none other than Claridge's, but a much earlier Claridge's, known as Mivart's. In Portsmouth, too, nothing remains of Nicholas's life with the Crummleses and their talented company. The old theatre in the High Street disappeared long before the George, Nelson's last lodging in England, was destroyed by bombs along with so much more of Portsmouth, and it is impossible to say where was 'the house of one Bulph, a pilot, in St Thomas's Street', graced by the portly presence of Mr and Mrs Crummles, or the tobacconist's shop on the Hard where Nicholas and Smike had rooms. The little cottage at Bow, which the Cheerybles obligingly let for a peppercorn rent to the Nicklebys, has been obliterated, like all other little cottages at Bow, by industrial development of a singularly hideous kind. The garden which Smike made 'a perfect wonder to look upon', wherein Mrs Nickleby was wooed by the gentleman in grey small-clothes with a shower of cucumbers and vegetable marrows, blooms now only in concrete.

7

Growing Fame

A family man of reasonable means, as Dickens had become in spite
of his youth, considered it essential to remove himself and his
household, lock, stock and barrel, to a holiday resort for the summer months. Summer in London was hot, dusty and 'gritty', as he
called it; besides, he liked a change of scene. In May 1839 he
rented Elm Cottage, Petersham. In the same year he was settling
his parents into a cottage in the West Country: his father's spendthrift habits continued to be an embarrassment to him, and his
relationship with his mother never seems to have recovered from
the blacking-factory episode. Mile End Cottage, Alphington, near
Exeter, seemed to him a place he could 'retire' them well out of his
own way, and one in which even his father would be unable to
spend much money. 'Exactly a mile beyond the city on the
Plymouth road there are two white cottages: one is theirs and the
other belongs to their landlady. I almost forget the number of
rooms; but there is an excellent parlour with two other rooms on
the ground-floor; there is really a beautiful little room over the
parlour which I am furnishing as a drawing-room, and there is a
splendid garden.' The rent was £20 a year, and he spent £70 on the
furnishings; cheap at the price, no doubt, to him. Mile End Cottage
survives in much-changed surroundings.

In 1837 he had taken Kate and the children to Broadstairs, a
small, pleasant resort on the Kent coast, hard by Ramsgate, and
liked it so much that it became for many years the Dickens family's

summer home. In 'Our English Watering-Place' in *Reprinted Pieces* he looked back affectionately to Broadstairs' gayer times:

'In truth, our watering-place itself has been left somewhat high and dry by the tide of years. Concerned as we are for its honour, we must reluctantly admit that the time when this pretty little semi-circular sweep of houses, tapering off at the end of the wooden pier into a point in the sea, was a gay place, and when the lighthouse overlooking it shone at daybreak on company dispersing from public balls, is but dimly traditional now.'

Their first lodging was at No. 12 High Street (now No. 31 and a shop), from which he wrote Forster an amusing letter about the nude bathing ('ladies and gentleman walking upon the earth in slippers of buff, and pickling themselves in the sea in complete suits of the same') and the neighbour who had 'a wife and something else under the same roof with the rest of his furniture—the wife deaf and blind, and the something else given to drinking'. He had discovered that the landlord of the Albion had delicious hollands, for which he had a taste but Forster had not. At the High Street house he worked on *Nicholas Nickleby* and *Oliver Twist*, and completed *Nicholas Nickleby* in 1839 at No. 40 Albion Street, two doors from the Albion Hotel, otherwise known as Ballards. (The house was later incorporated in the hotel, which remembers his visits in its decorations.) In 1840 he was writing to Maclise, in facetious imitation of Byron:

> *My foot is in the house,*
> *My bath is in the sea,*
> *And before I take a souse,*
> *Here's a single note to thee.*

He was trying hard to get a lease of Fort House, which stood on the cliff at the north end of Broadstairs in a fine airy position, with a cornfield between it and the sea. But in 1840 it was not yet his and he had to be content with Lawn House, Albion Street, where he wrote part of *Barnaby Rudge* and *The Old Curiosity Shop*. At last 'the residence' he most desired passed into his keeping, and from his 'airy nest' he was able to enjoy the summer and autumn for many years. Here he wrote busily, paused to look out of the window of the little study at the sea winking like a sleepy lion, the fishing-boats 'dancing like mad', the butterflies fluttering: all the 'brilliancy out of doors' which lured the Inimitable so much that he 'breaketh off, rusheth to the machines, and plungeth into the sea'. He, who had always been fascinated by moving waters, now almost owned a piece of the sea itself. Lovingly he described it, brought the very salt breath of it to less fortunate friends in London, enjoyed himself with all the zest of which he was capable. Domestic shadows may have hovered even here, but the tone of all his letters from Broadstairs suggests that residence there brought him a lightness of spirit he did not feel in London.

The little town of Broadstairs is still a graceful crescent round golden sands, rare on the Kent shore. 'At bathing-time . . . the little bay re-echoes with every shrill variety of shriek and splash' from adults as well as the hordes of children for whom the place seemed too small even in Dickens's time. Rebuilding has largely spared Broadstairs. Fort House is a Dickens memorial, though it has been much altered and was renamed Bleak House in his life-time. It has, in fact, no connection with the novel, other than that its outline was planned there: the name seems to have arisen from its geographical situation having earned it the reputation of being a bleak house indeed. The little Regency villa which the Dickenses knew was later 'improved' by one of those builders who went round the Kent coast at the turn of the century transforming in-offensive private residences into imitation castles with square battlements. A west wing was added in 1901 and is now the private residence of the family of the late Charles Eade, who bought the house in 1958 and collected the numerous Dickensian relics which are now to be seen in this most appropriate setting.

Dickens's bedroom, study and dining-room are all as he would have known them. The study ('about the size of a warm bath') is the most important of the rooms, for in it he wrote most of *David Copperfield* and plotted out *Bleak House*. It holds his desk chair, which may or not be the same as the chair in Luke Fildes's painting *The Empty Chair*, and the drawing-cabinet designed and used by his friend and illustrator George Cruikshank. The ornate brass bed in Dickens's bedroom was brought from the principal bedroom of the Bull at Rochester, where tradition says Dickens often slept in it, as, it is said, did Queen Victoria, though the bed appears to be of later date than her visit. The relics and portraits elsewhere displayed are only rivalled by the collection at 48 Doughty Street. There is a feeling of lightness and pleasure pervading the house, in spite of its grim exterior, as though Dickens's enjoyment and affection had impressed themselves on it in defiance of builders and time. 'It is more delightful here than I can express . . . O it is wonderful!'

Broadstairs is proud of Dickens. A Dickens pub has an Oliver Twist bar for children; plaques abound, even one facetiously pointing out that Dickens did *not* live there. Another inn which does not advertise the association, though it was in fact his local when he lived at Fort House, is the Tartar Frigate, on the point which curves round to the harbour. He called it 'the cosiest little sailor's inn . . . that is to be met around the coast. . . . The very walls have long ago learned "Tom Bowling" and "The Bay of Biscay" by heart and would be thankful for a fresh song'. The walls, unfortunately, threatened to collapse some years ago because of the rat-runs with which they were honeycombed, so that the brewers were obliged to rebuild the façade. But in spite of this, and of the somewhat overpoweringly 'antique' décor, it retains a salty charm and a feeling of Dickensian bonhomie highly conducive to the consumption of beer and crab sandwiches. Little deductive power is needed to infer that Mr Tartar, ex-R.N., the handsome and breezy sailor who wins Rosa Bud's heart in *Edwin Drood*, got his name from the inn.

A pretty balconied house in Nuckall's Place, looking out to sea, bears the name of Dickens House. There lived in it one Mary Strong, confidently said by Charles Dickens the Younger to have been the original of David Copperfield's formidable aunt, Betsey Trotwood; she was certainly a similarly violent enemy of donkey-riders. With equal confidence Dickensian inquirers have identified the house as that in which the exhausted and footsore David at last found his aunt, though he describes it as 'a very neat little cottage', whilst Dickens House runs to three storeys and a pair of attics which are named David and Janet, after the Copperfield characters. There is indeed 'a little piece of green' in front of the house, now enclosed and no longer vulnerable to the depredations of donkey-riders. But there stands near by, in the holiday season, one of those grotesquely cheerful plush animals on which children are sometimes persuaded to sit for their photographs at seaside resorts; by a happy chance, it is a donkey.

Even the giants of Dickensian research have not discovered why Dickens transferred the house and Miss Trotwood to Dover. That town was hardly known to Dickens, except as a gateway to the

Continent, until three years after he had written *David Copperfield*. But on a shop at the corner of the market-place a tablet tells interested persons that:

Here

is the site of the steps

on which

Charles Dickens

represents

David Copperfield

as resting in his

search for his aunt

Betsey Trotwood

From Broadstairs, over the years, Dickens explored and enjoyed the Isle of Thanet. A strange region, it differs ineffably from 'Garden-of-England' Kent. Wide, stark, it is as though the vanished Wantsum channel, the Roman waterway which made it an island, still flows, keeping it in a kind of isolation, despite flats and factories and a hoverport. The old, lovely Margate Theatre, where Dickens saw the tragedy *The Athenian Captive* wildly burlesqued, has descended to bingo and is understandably haunted by the ghost of its great actress-manageress, Sarah Thorne. Ramsgate, where the Tuggses revelled, has some fine Georgian crescents and rows of those houses which Dickens despised so much: 'One ground-floor sitting-room, and three cells with beds in them. A double-house. Family on the opposite side.' It is as well to go and see them before they all disappear; though he did not appreciate their grace, we can.

However alluring Broadstairs might be, Dickens's work lay mainly in London. The house in Doughty Street saw his swift rise to fame after the publication of *The Pickwick Papers*, *Oliver Twist* and *Nicholas Nickleby*. Here he held conferences with publishers and illustrators, gave the evening parties in which he revelled, and wrote in the first-floor study overlooking the garden. Here two daughters were born, Mamie and Katey, and Dickens felt that a larger house was needed for his too-rapidly growing family. The

80

item which appears on his cheque-book counterfoil for 28th December 1839 was to be a more frequent entry than he liked; it read: 'Mrs Havercombe (Monthly Nurse), £4.11.0.'

A month earlier he had written to his friend Macready: 'You must come and see my new house when we have it to rights.' The new house was No. 1 Devonshire Terrace, York Gate, at the corner of Marylebone High Street and Marylebone Road (then known as the New Road), facing the York Gate into Regent's Park. He referred to it in *The Uncommercial Traveller* as 'a house which then appeared to me to be a frightfully first-class Family Mansion, involving awful responsibilities'.

One of the present authors lived in this house some years ago, and still recalls vividly, and with a melancholy pleasure, its charms. It was no longer detached, as it had been in 1839, and was higher by one storey, which had been rather clumsily added. Other changes had been made in the course of its conversion into an apartment-house and, indeed, in those days nearly every room had a separate tenant, so that it was impossible to inspect them all. But a great deal was visible, and was as Dickens knew it: 'He cared most for Devonshire Terrace, perhaps for the bit of ground attached to it', said Forster. A graceful staircase curved upwards from the hall with its polished mahogany doors; the drawing-room had a fine mantelpiece of Italian marble, said to have been installed by Dickens, and an ornate plaster ceiling. The smaller room looking out onto the garden had (if memory serves) a french window with a step or two leading down to the lawn. This seems to be confirmed by Mamie Dickens's description of it as 'a pretty room, with steps leading directly into the garden from it, and with an extra baize door to keep out all sounds and noise'. This garden, a great improvement on that which he had left at Doughty Street, was a great joy to the young man who loved to play battledore and shuttlecock with his children and bowls with his friends, to walk, meditate, or amuse himself with Grip, the pet talking raven.* Longfellow wrote to a friend in 1841: 'I write this from Dickens's study, the focus from which so many luminous things have radiated. The raven croaks in the garden, and the ceaseless roar of London fills my ears.'

* Grip's stuffed remains were sold, at the Gadshill sale after his master's death, for £127: a somewhat grisly portrait of him can be seen at the Leather Bottle, Cobham.

A century later the garden had declined into a mangy, sour patch of weeds and bare earth, though one or two plane-trees remained on the side adjoining the church of St Marylebone, which he was to use as the scene of little Paul Dombey's burial and Mr Dombey's second marriage. The staircase, with its charming empty niche (where who knows which of Dickens's 'dainty and useful ornaments' had stood? Or, perhaps 'a vase of bright and fresh flowers' such as always adorned his study table?) seemed, as it wound upwards to the nursery floor, to be that very same staircase on which the ruined Dombey had seen the vision of his lost daughter: *

'He stopped, looking up towards the skylight; and a figure, childish itself, but carrying a child, and singing as it went, seemed to be there again. Anon, it was the same figure, alone, stopping for an instant, with suspended breath; the bright hair clustering loosely round its tearful face; and looking back at him.'

In 1958 demolition gangs arrived at the pretty house in Devonshire Terrace. They tore it down, together with its neighbours and the little Church House which, close by St Marylebone Church, had stood among green lawns haunted by bold blackbirds, like a country vicarage. Bulldozers uprooted the garden, muckshifters removed every trace of the building which had seen the flowering of a genius more bright and fresh than any bloom on that study table; which had seen the writing of most of *Dombey and Son*, *The Old Curiosity Shop*, *Barnaby Rudge*, *A Christmas Carol*, *The Cricket on the Hearth*, *Martin Chuzzlewit* and *David Copperfield*, and which, incidentally, had been eminently habitable and had housed a dance-studio as well as tenants. Protests and petitions from the Dickens Fellowship and others were in vain; Dickens's house was replaced by a large office block, featureless but for an unusual degree of ugliness and, in the entrance, a bas-relief depicting Dickens and some of his characters—a somewhat belated and ineffectual gesture towards his memory.

Perhaps because it saw the last of his treasured youth (he was twenty-seven when he took it and thirty-nine when he left it) the house became to him, as some houses do, irreplaceable, forever lamented. In 1844, away from it only for a time, in Italy, he wrote to Forster: 'I seem as if I had plucked myself out of my proper

* See footnote on page 94.

82

soil when I left Devonshire Terrace, and would take root no more until I return to it. . . . Did I tell you how many fountains we have here? No matter. If they played nectar they wouldn't please me half so well as the West Middlesex Waterworks at Devonshire Terrace.'

Because of the Dickenses' long absences at Broadstairs and on the Continent during these years, the house was frequently let. Sometimes when they returned 'the dear old home' was still occupied by tenants, and they had to wait temporarily in other premises. One of these lodgings was 9 Osnaburgh Terrace, off Euston Road, near Holy Trinity Church, with its entrance in Albany Street; another, close by, was in Chester Place (the number is unknown). The Bedford Hotel at Brighton and the long-demolished Euston and Victoria Hotel in Euston Square also served as 'temporary encampments' during these peregrinations. The restlessness of Victorian families, the problems of luggage, children and staff, were exemplified and intensified in this household, whose head was as volatile as a shooting star.

Although he was now a seasoned traveller in America, France, Italy and Switzerland, and devoted whole volumes, such as *American Notes* and *Pictures from Italy*, to some of his journeys abroad, the England of his reporting days was still the main source of backgrounds to his novels. *The Old Curiosity Shop* rambles up to the Midlands along the coach routes he himself had taken, but first the story must be established in London.

Where was the Old Curiosity Shop itself? Not, alas, in Portsmouth Street, to the east of Southampton Row, where unwitting visitors come to take photographs of an attractive little antique shop bearing the inscription 'Immortalized by Charles Dickens'. A Mr Charles Tesseyman wrote to the *Echo* in 1883 a letter admitting that his brother, who had occupied 14 Portsmouth Street from 1868 to 1877, had had the words 'The Old Curiosity Shop' placed on the shop-front for purely business purposes—'he being a dealer in books, paintings, old China, etc. Before 1868 . . . no suggestion had ever been made that the place was the veritable Old Curiosity Shop immortalized by Dickens. After my brother's death in 1877, the present tenant had my brother's name painted out, but left standing the words 'The Old Curiosity Shop'— doubtless with a shrewd eye to business. An American writer, visiting the old house, I think in 1881, and seeing the inscription, had his imagination fired with thoughts of Little Nell and Kit, and Dick Swiveller and Quilp, and straightway wrote an article in *Scribner's Monthly* in which he assured his readers that this was the old original Old Curiosity Shop of Dickens.'

So legends are begun. Where the actual shop was, if it ever existed, is debatable. Georgina Hogarth told the actor Sir John Hare that it was in Green Street (now Irving Street), at the back of the National Portrait Gallery. No trace of this exists; some baths were built over the site of whatever used to be there. Nearly all the other London sites mentioned in *The Old Curiosity Shop* went long ago: Quilp's home on Tower Hill, the sinister wharf where his counting-house stood (the warehouse buildings of Butler's Wharf have risen instead); Dick Swiveller's lodging in Drury Lane; Sampson Brass's home in Bevis Marks. Farther north—in the country, as it then was—Abel Cottage, the home of the Garlands and their agreeable pony, may be one of those small eighteenth-century houses which, wearing a plaintively rural air, huddle anxiously on the west side of the Finchley Road, waiting for the hammer and the bulldozer.

The epic journey of Little Nell and her grandfather is, very oddly, completely without geographical identifications, even in the form of disguised names. For some reason Dickens decided to let the reader work it out for himself. Various eager and erudite Dickensians have done this, with slightly contradictory results. Percy Fitzgerald, whose zeal knew no bounds, deduced it thus: starting out that June morning by way of Tottenham Court Road the old traveller and the young one passed through Islington 'where faded gentility essayed to make its last stand' (and to which gentility has returned with a vengeance today), or possibly along Oxford Street and the Edgware Road to Finchley. By breakfast time they were on a hill, either at Hampstead or Highgate. Cattermole's illustration shows them resting beneath an oak on what looks like Parliament Hill. The little town with the old grey church, where they met Codlin and Short, the Punch and Judy men, seemed to Fitzgerald to be Bushey, a place now submerged in brick. Four days' march later they came to a race town which may have been Warwick. The town at which they arrived as part of Mrs Jarley's waxwork entourage is identified as Coventry; it would have grieved Fitzgerald, and even more Dickens, to see in the future the fate of those 'houses of stone, houses of red brick, houses of lath and

84

plaster, and houses of wood . . . little winking windows and low-arched doors', and that of the people who were living in them, on a certain terrible night of November 1940 when the bombers came.

After escaping from the town and its gambling hazards, the two reached the banks of the Warwickshire and Birmingham Canal and proceeded to travel by boat to Birmingham where, after their strange, brilliantly described interlude in industrial England, they moved on towards an ancient town full of half-timbered houses. Fitzgerald thinks this was Bridgenorth, or Shrewsbury, where Dickens had spent a night in 1838, staying at the Lion, which like much of the town retains its black-and-white beauty. The letter he wrote from there to Kate gives a brief, vivid word-picture of the 'miles of cinderpaths and blazing furnaces and roaring steam-engines . . . and such a mass of dirt gloom and misery'* which he used as the background to Nell's sojourn in Birmingham.

The pilgrimage, and Nell's life, end at the village of Tong in Shropshire, according to Fitzgerald. Dickens told Archdeacon Lloyd that he had gone over from Shrewsbury especially to see Tong, its celebrated castle and church, a fine piece of Early Perpendicular with its central octagonal tower. He describes it without his usual contempt for antiquity, with a lingering emotion; for throughout the novel he is working his way towards death, a painful but to him necessary re-enactment of the death of Mary Hogarth. Tong Church is the culmination of his symbolic journey. 'The old grey porch, the mullioned windows, the venerable grave-stones dotting the green churchyard, the ancient tower, the very weathercock; the brown thatched roofs of cottage, barn, and homestead, peeping from among the trees; the stream that rippled by the distant water-mill; the blue Welsh mountains far away . . . a very aged, ghostly place; the church had . . . once had a convent or monastery attached; for arches in ruins, remains of oriel windows, and fragments of blackened walls, were yet standing.'

The church is a strikingly beautiful building, with something exotic and fantastic in its design; though nothing like as fantastic as Cattermole's drawing of the exterior, which gives it an air of crazy decrepitude and decay. Possibly it looked something like that in 1838; it was heavily restored in 1892 and appears good for another thousand years or so of life. The interior is rich in beauty,

---

* *Letters of Charles Dickens*, Pilgrim Edition, edited by Madeline House and Graham Storey, vol. i, 1820–39, page 447 (Clarendon Press, 1965).

with its famous Vernon Chantry, the 'Golden Chapel', original choirstalls and painted screens. Cattermole makes it into something like a film set; but then, when Dickens describes Nell's bedroom as 'a kind of closet, where I saw a little bed that a fairy might have slept in, it looked so very small', Cattermole places her in a sizable half-tester within a high-ceilinged room crammed with every variety of junk, from a suit of armour downwards. The mirror by her bed is even a resting-place for what looks like, but surely cannot be, a fireman's helmet.

The 'two small dwellings with sunken windows and oaken doors', in one of which the kindly schoolmaster housed Nell and the old man, 'have since fallen into complete ruin', said Fitzgerald. In fact, these pretty little Elizabethan dwellings still stand, happily restored and in private ownership. The little inn where the schoolmaster had proposed to leave Nell and her grandfather while he made inquiries in the village was the Old Bell, now a farm; its name has been passed on to another inn near by.

A claim to be the 'Little Nell' church is also made by Minster-in-Thanet on behalf of its lovely Norman abbey with the little Saxon tower beside it. Like Tong, it is richly ornamented, full of legend. But how could Dickens have resisted a ghoulish reference to the tale of the burning of the Saxon church by the Danes, who first imprisoned in it the folk of Minster, the priests and the nuns? For Tong he invented three facetious legends of a wicked baron, a miser, and 'a grey-haired lady who had been hanged and drawn and quartered by glorious Queen Bess', sublimely unaware that this unpleasant fate was never inflicted on women. Minster, to which Dickens must have driven or walked from Broadstairs, is well worth a visit for its own sake, and deserves its share of Dickensian association. But it was Tong Church that Cattermole drew, and within living memory an ancient verger delighted to lead visitors to inspect 'Little Nell's Grave'.

The terrain of *Barnaby Rudge* is specifically identified by Dickens, but would be hard to explore now. The London inns and houses were of the eighteenth century, already old when Dickens wrote that novel, and doomed to vanish, even if Hitler had not removed them. Gabriel Varden's neat house in Clerkenwell—'on the shady side of the way, for good housewives know that sunlight damages their cherished furniture'—belonged to the days when Clerkenwell was still part rural, a place of fields and gardens, the

New River flowing above ground and respectable middle-class folk plying their trades in the modest houses and shops of that historic quarter of London. Only the splendid gateway of the priory of the Knights of St John of Jerusalem and the graceful Sessions House on the green remain of the Clerkenwell Dickens knew; and of those the Sessions House is too recent to recall the Vardens. Anyone desiring a sight of the rooms where Mr Chester resided in cynical elegance may find them at Paper Buildings, King's Bench Walk, which was spared from the destruction which overtook much of the Temple. The house where that sad, misguided man Lord George Gordon addressed the mob still stands in sober Welbeck Street; but the Boot, behind the Foundling Hospital, where the rioters met to plan desperate deeds in the cause of the Protestant Association of England, has gone. Dickens knew the Boot well, but the inn which was almost his local when he lived at Doughty Street was only built in 1801.

The heart of the novel lies in one building in which the story begins and ends: the Maypole Inn at Chigwell, Essex. On this building the whole plot depends: it is the stage set on which the main action takes place, other scenes being played before the curtain. Presided over by John Willet, the slow, obstinate, bucolic landlord, it is the focal point, the centre of the web for all the threads spun by the spider Dickens: the Rudge murder mystery, beginning with the wonderful, eerie tale of Solomon Daisy—'it belongs to this house, and nobody but Solomon Daisy has ever told it under this roof, or ever shall, what's more'; the duel between John Chester and Geoffrey Haredale; the plot against the love of Edward Chester and Haredale's niece Emma; the passion of Joe Willet for Dolly Varden, and the more violent passion for her entertained by poor brutal 'Maypole Hugh'. Here come Lord George and his minions on their 'No Popery' crusade which ends in the Gordon riots, and in those riots the Maypole is ravaged and spoiled: 'the sanctuary, the mystery, the hallowed ground: here it was, crammed with men, clubs, sticks, torches, pistols . . . smoking private and personal pipes, cutting down the sacred grove of lemons, hacking and hewing of the celebrated cheese . . . noise, smoke, light, darkness, frolic, anger, laughter, groans, plunder, fear and ruin.' John Willet was never quite the same man again, but his inn was made of sterner stuff. Joe and Dolly restored and reopened it, and 'it was a long time . . . before there was such a country inn as the Maypole, in all England'.

The Maypole was, in fact, the King's Head, Chigwell. For some reason Dickens gave it the name of quite another inn at Chigwell Row, some two miles away. He was fond of the inn and the village, then a 'rural and retired' place on the edge of Epping Forest. 'Chigwell, my dear fellow,' he wrote to Forster, 'is the greatest place in the world. Name your day for going. Such a delicious old inn opposite the churchyard, such a lovely ride, such beautiful forest scenery, such an out-of-the-way rural place; such a sexton! I say again, name your day.' Forster recorded: 'His promise was exceeded by our enjoyment; and his delight in the double recognition of himself and of *Barnaby* by the landlord of the nice old inn, far exceeded any pride he would have taken in what the world thinks the highest sort of honour.'

Cattermole, the illustrator of *Barnaby Rudge*, turned the 'nice old inn' into a wild Gothic fantasy belonging to no known architectural style. He had preserved a certain semblance of reality in his drawing of Tong Church, but at Chigwell his romantic imagination ran riot. Perhaps the 'steaming grog' whose scent had so beguiled Gabriel Varden was of an unusual potency, leaving Cattermole with the impression that the King's Head was twice or three times as large and a hundred times more fantastic than the reality. His portrait of it is extraordinarily charming and fits, in a curious way, Dickens's lingering, rhapsodic description of the house 'with its overhanging stories, drowsy little panes of glass, and front bulging out and projecting over the pathway . . . its windows were old diamond-paned lattices, its floors were sunken and uneven, its ceilings blacked by the hand of Time, and heavy with massive beams. Over the doorway was an ancient porch, quaintly and grotesquely carved.'

It was old, decrepit, decayed, unhygienic, but Dickens loved it. He would be glad to see it standing today as sturdily as ever, opposite the churchyard where Barnaby and his mother sat on a tombstone and ate their lunch. Its plain, plastered front is nothing like that shown by Cattermole, but is none the less unspoiled and attractive, the upper storeys leaning out to shelter the entering traveller, the diamond-paned windows still twinkling sleepily in the sun. He would be pleased to find himself and *Barnaby Rudge* remembered there. In 1899 'the Charles Dickens Lodge' was consecrated at the King's Head, and it is a perfect spot for the attentions of Dickensian pilgrims today. In the 'Chester Room' upstairs may be had those dinners (though perhaps not 'dressed upon the shortest notice') whose 'gentle sound of frying, with musical clatter of plates and dishes, and a savoury smell that made even the boisterous wind a perfume' was so fatal to Gabriel Varden's resolution to pass by the Maypole. Now, as then, on a winter night, the cold black country seems to frown you off and drive you for a refuge into the tavern's hospitable arms. In summer the garden at the back is full of flowers and children. One of the present authors, sitting there in sunshine with a tankard, watching her small son tear along the low wall proclaiming, with appropriate sounds, that he was an aeroplane, reflected that the shade of Dickens, though he would approve the unchanged aspect of his beloved 'Maypole', would approve its changes even more.

Solomon Daisy, short Tom Cobb the general chandler, and long Phil Parkes the ranger might feel a trifle out of place in the refurbished inn-parlour, with its bars and pretty barmaid, its snacks and sophisticated drinks, but they would soon settle down, recognizing the old, familiar room, which still retains 'its heavy timbers and panelled walls'. A portrait of the man who created the characters hangs over the main bar, and in a little room leading out of the parlour is a framed document at which Dickensians must pause. It is a proposal for insurance, addressed to the Sun Life Assurance Society by one Charles Dickens, aged next birthday 26, present residence 48 Doughty Street: suggested sum, £1,000; term, life. Mr Dickens's usual Medical Attendant is F. Pickthorn Esq., of St John's Wood, his non-medical referee John Forster Esq., of 58 Lincoln's Inn Fields. Mr Dickens is requested to inform the Society whether he has ever had Gout, Asthma, or any Fit: whether he is afflicted with Rupture or has any symptoms of Consumption of the Lungs or any other disorder tending to shorten life. Mr Dickens replies that he is free from all such afflictions, but admits to having had Cowpox. The date is 9th January 1838.

A Victorian addition at the side of the inn would have given Dickens immense pleasure. It is a commodious private theatre, in which the late Bransby Williams used to give his Dickensian character performances. Empty when last seen, with that air of desolation peculiar to unused theatres, it seemed to be waiting for

89

Dickens's lively troup of amateur barnstormers to bring it to life with *Every Man in his Humour*.

Across the road, in the churchyard, is a tombstone which gives the strolling visitor food for speculation. It commemorates a small boy who died in 1862, and whose name was John William Jasper. Dickens, with his well-known propensity for revisiting old haunts, may—just possibly—have returned to Chigwell in the 1860s, and may—just possibly—have remembered little John Jasper's name when he sought for one to fit the uncle of Edwin Drood.

8

Devonshire Terrace: Life and Writing

When Dickens did not name a locality, or disguise it thinly so that it might, so to speak, be unmasked at midnight, he set for posterity another hurdle in the ever-delightful guessing game which we never tire of playing with the works of popular if enigmatic authors. Did Shakespeare really mean Wilmcote, his mother's native village, when in *The Taming of the Shrew* he made Christopher Sly refer to Marian Hacket, the fat ale-wife of Wincot? How could Sherlock Holmes, Dr Watson and Sir Henry Baskerville have taken the 10.30 a.m. train from Paddington to reach Baskerville Hall on Dartmoor, when it was in fact a non-stop from Exeter to Plymouth, with no Dartmoor connection? Similarly, where was the Blue Dragon Inn of *Martin Chuzzlewit*, in the 'little Wiltshire village within easy journey of the fair old town of Salisbury'?

It is a charming inn: Dickens seems to have had a peculiar propensity for inns at this time of his life (1843). He described lovingly the faded, ancient dragon of the sign, who was yet courteous and considerate, too: 'for in the midst of his rampant feebleness he kept one of his fore-paws near his nose, as though he would say "Don't mind me—it's only my fun", while he held out the other in polite and hospitable entreaty.' Unfortunately Dickens omitted to say where the Blue Dragon was. There is no Blue Dragon in the Salisbury region, though there is a Green Dragon at Alderbury, three miles from the town on the Southampton Road. The Green

Dragon was 'a village ale-house' in Dickens's day, a description which fits its Blue counterpart; but it was too small to have accommodated old Chuzzlewit and his army of expectant relations, a formidable crew to descend on any inn. Dickensian savants have in the main rejected it in favour of the George Inn, Amesbury, eight miles to the north of Salisbury. By Amesbury, in coaching days, went the famous 'Quicksilver' Exeter Mail to and from London, and the George (whose connection with Dragons is fairly clear) was a large coaching-inn capable of putting up Pecksniffs, Chuzzlewits and Spottletoes. It was discovered by H. Snowden Ward that the turnpike house where Tom Pinch left his box still existed at Amesbury, and that the church where he played the organ was in the right place. In spite of these finds, a rival Dickensian, Robert Allbut, refuted the coach-route clue and declared that the Lion's Head, Middle Winterslow, was the genuine Blue Dragon, that Tom played the organ of All Saints' Church there, and that Clarendon Park, between Winterslow and Salisbury, then less a park than a wood, was the scene of Jonas Chuzzlewit's murder of Montague Tigg.

The probable solution to the mystery is that the Blue Dragon was a composite portrait of several inns. Whatever the truth, Amesbury lies on a pleasant road across Salisbury Plain and makes a good halting-place on the way from east to west. It does not matter greatly that its church has a square tower instead of the spire Dickens mentioned; he also talked about the 'towers' of Salisbury Cathedral coming into view, though a moment's thought would have told him that the sky-piercing spire of Salisbury is, like God in the counting-song, 'all alone, and ever more shall be so'.

Salisbury itself is still 'a fair old town', still has a market-day when it is crowded with 'young farmers and old farmers' and their wives, though the latter no longer wear beaver bonnets and red cloaks, or ride 'shaggy horses purged of all earthly passions'. Instead, the Salburians and their visitors throng the narrow old streets round the Poultry Cross, where Richard III's Buckingham died by the axe, in a variety of mechanized vehicles which would have charmed Dickens, and earthly passions are not absent from the scene, particularly in traffic jams.

The lodging of the Misses Pecksniff in London is beyond identification, though Robert Allbut thought that it was in King's Head Court, Fish Street Hill, from the top of a house in which the

21

The King's Head, Chigwell, Essex: the Maypole Inn of Barnaby Rudge.

22

The George Inn, Amesbury, often said to be the original of the Blue Dragon in Martin Chuzzlewit. *Engraving by C. G. Harper.*

The Rookery, Blunderstone:
Miss Trotwood peers in at Clara Copperfield.
Illustration by 'Phiz' to David Copperfield.

24

The 'great foolish image . . . blowing a dry shell'
(from David Copperfield) in the New Kent Road.

Tulkinghorn's House, Lincoln's Inn Fields, London,
in Bleak House. John Forster, Dickens's biographer
and friend, lived in half of it.

26

*Chesney Wold, country home of the Dedlocks
in* Bleak House: *'Phiz' evidently preferred
this to a realistic representation of
Rockingham Castle.*

27

Poor Jo points out to Lady Dedlock the grave of her lover in the 'hemmed-in churchyard, pestiferous and obscene' which was the burial-ground of St Mary-le-Strand. Illustration by 'Phiz' to Bleak House.

*Knebworth House, Hertfordshire, the home of
Sir Edward Bulwer-Lytton, where Dickens indulged
his passion for private theatricals.*

Monument 'was close beside you, with every hair erect upon his golden head', a description which recurs whenever one glimpses that fiery finial. 'Todger's', wherever it was, is almost certainly no more. From Fish Street Hill has departed forever the shade of 'Pecksniff the sire . . . the Architect, Artist and Man', while the jilted Charity lingers only as a fainting form in bridal satin; and poor silly Merry has departed, as she left the sighing young men of Todger's, leaving but the memory of 'a skip and a shape'.

Time has not, on the whole, been kind to the settings of *Martin Chuzzlewit*. In Kingsgate Street, High Holborn, the home of Sairey Gamp was one of the more interesting residences in the neighbourhood, being over the shop of Poll Sweedlepipe the bird-fancier, 'next door but one to the celebrated mutton-pie shop, and directly opposite to the original cat's-meat warehouse'. It vanished in 1902 with the building of Kingsway. The only scene in the book which can be in any way re-created today is that set in Temple Court, where John Westlock wooed Ruth Pinch, while the fountain played in the sun 'until the dimples, merging into one another, swelled into a general smile, that covered the whole surface of the basin', and Ruth blushed 'to a terrible extent' beneath her brown bonnet. 'They had no more to do with the Fountain, bless you, than they had with—with Love, or any out of the way thing of that sort.'

The *Christmas Books*, published between 1843 and 1848, are scantily localized. An old knocker in Craven Street, Strand, used to be pointed out as the very one which suggested to Dickens the transmogrification of Scrooge's knocker into Marley's dead face; but, says legend, the request of an enterprising photographer for the permission of the owner to photograph her knocker led to her removing it and placing it in her bank for safe keeping. Bob Cratchit's humble home in Camden Town may have been a memory of Dickens's life in Bayham Street. *The Chimes*, successor to *A Christmas Carol*, was possibly put into Dickens's mind by the bells of St Dunstan in the West, whose lantern, the crown of Fleet Street, must have drawn his eyes many a time as he drove down the street on journalistic business. It is certainly the tower of Maclise's illustration. It was a new church in his day, built in 1831–3, and therefore to be admired. He remembered the old church, and the best-known clock in London, with the two giant-figures striking the quarters. Cowper compared their action to the laboured efforts of dull poets:

> *Beating alternately in measured time*
> *The clockwork tintinnabulum of rhyme.*

Dickens had mentioned these figures before—Maypole Hugh heard the giants strike upon the bell before he knocked at Middle Temple Gate, and David Copperfield, who was a boy when Dickens was a boy, paused in passing 'to catch them at it', as one pauses now in Piccadilly to catch in motion the elegant puppets adorning the façade of Messrs Fortnum and Mason. He could not mention them in *The Chimes*, for when the old church was pulled down in 1830 the giants were banished to the villa of the Marquis of Hertford in Regent's Park, and did not return home until 1935. They, and the figures of King Lud and his sons, and the statue of Queen Elizabeth, all survived the Great Fire of 1666 and that other one of 1940.

On the whole, *The Chimes* has more of a provincial than an urban air, like *The Cricket on the Hearth*, which could have been set in any of the areas of outer London so well known to Dickens: Barnet, perhaps, or his favourite, St Albans.

With *Dombey and Son* he returned to the London townscape he knew so well, beginning the story on his own doorstep in Marylebone. If the Dombey house is not 1 Devonshire Terrace, it is very near*; a house at the corner of Mansfield Street and Queen Anne Street has been suggested as answering its description. If it were so, the Dombey family would perhaps have attended All Souls, Langham Place, rather than St Marylebone Church. It would be entertaining to know Mr Dombey's opinion of the area now, with its population of distinguished medical men of the Doctor Parker Peps *genre* ('one of the Court Physicians, and a man of immense reputation for assisting at the increase of great families'), of B.B.C. personnel on their way to work or lunch, and of prosperous flat-dwellers. Miss Lucretia Tox could no longer afford to inhabit that 'dark little house, that had been squeezed, in some remote period of English History, into a fashionable neighbourhood at the west end of the town . . . it was not exactly in a court, and it

---

* The 1969 B.B.C. television serialization of *Dombey and Son* reproduced almost exactly the hall and staircase at Devonshire Terrace as those of Dombey's house.

was not exactly in a yard . . . the name of this retirement, where grass grew between the chinks in the stone pavement, was Princess's Place, and in Princess's Place was Princess's Chapel, with a tinkling bell'. Miss Tox dwelt in what would now be known as a mews flat or maisonette, now more fashionable than the great houses around it, and beyond the means of such impoverished single ladies. With old Joey Bagstock she would be forced to seek lodgings far from Marylebone.

The chapel with the tinkling bell may have been St Mary's, Wyndham Place, whose bell still chimes the quarters with maddening persistence. The Princess's Arms, 'much resorted to by splendid footmen', is unidentifiable, but the Marylebone streets are rich in pubs known to Dickens. The Dover Castle, in a mews near the junction of New Cavendish Street and Portland Place, is typical of them.

It must have been a joyful release to Dickens to move from scenes set in the West End to the London riverside he loved so much. Here he was at home, back in his boyhood visiting Christopher Huffam in Limehouse, smelling the ineffable smells of the water and the ships and the merchandise, seaman's 'baccy and tar, rum and sugar. With what zest he writes of the situation of the offices of Dombey and Son, in a district full of 'hints of adventurous and romantic story. . . . Gog and Magog held their state within ten minutes' walk; the Royal Exchange was close to hand; the Bank of England, with its vaults of gold and silver "down among the dead men" underground, was their magnificent neighbour. Just round the corner stood the rich East India House, teeming with suggestions of precious stuffs and stones, tigers, elephants, howdahs, hookahs, umbrellas, palm trees, palanquins, and gorgeous princes of a brown complexion sitting on carpets, with their slippers very much turned up at the toes. Anywhere in the immediate vicinity there might be seen pictures of ships speeding away full sail to all parts of the world; outfitting warehouses ready to pack off anybody anywhere, fully equipped in half an hour; and little timber midshipmen in obsolete naval uniforms, eternally employed outside the shopdoors of nautical instrument-makers in taking observations of the hackney coaches'.

The description points to somewhere very close to the junction of Poultry, Cornhill, and the other six streets which meet at the present Bank underground station. Perhaps Dombey and Son had their offices in Lombard Street (of Beadnell memory) or Walbrook. The little shop of Sol Gills the instrument-maker is not to be found today, but the figure of the Little Midshipman, his shop-sign, has been preserved in Dickens House and is one of its most charming exhibits, a smart little fellow in the uniform of Nelson's navy, or earlier. It used to stand outside the shop of Norie and Wilson at 156 Minories, and before that outside their premises at 157 Leadenhall Street, where Dickens probably saw it 'taking observations of the hackney coaches'.

No. 9 Brig Place, where Captain Cuttle lodged at Mrs Mac-Stinger's in what was 'at once a first floor and a top storey', is not to be found, any more than Brig Place itself. It was 'on the brink of a little canal near the India Docks, where there was a swivel bridge which opened now and then to let some wandering monster of a ship come roaming up the street like a stranded leviathan'. Such 'rows of houses, with little vane-surmounted masts uprearing themselves from among the scarlet beans', have long disappeared from the East India Dock region. A drive to Greenwich, keeping close to the river where possible and taking in the Ratcliff Highway, will give a fair idea of what they were like in their prime. Such as remain today have fallen into sad squalor and decay, and pollard willows and scarlet beans no longer flourish among them.

The Little Midshipman's shop is the eastern focus of *Dombey and Son*, as the gloomy house in Marylebone is the western focus. Other localities are incidental, the product of Dickens's travelling. Little Paul Dombey went to school in Brighton because Dickens had stayed there in 1837 and 1841, at the Old Ship Hotel in King's Road, and in 1847 he was working on *Dombey and Son* at 148 King's Road, next to the Norfolk Hotel.* Dr Blimber's school was nowhere in particular, but Chichester House, at the corner of Chichester Terrace, near Sussex Square, was once a school, and Harrison Ainsworth thought it the original of Blimber's. Little Paul's lodging at Mrs Pipchin's 'castle', in 'a steep by-street at Brighton, where the soil was more than usually chalky, flinty, and sterile, and the houses were more than usually brittle and thin', may have been in one of the narrow streets which rush downhill from Queen's Road towards the Pavilion and the Lanes. Dickens

* In 1848 he and Kate were at the Bedford Hotel, where Mr Dombey also put up, and he used the hotel thereafter during reading tours.

liked Brighton, finding it then as now 'a gay place for a week or so' and 'a bright change'.

Leamington, where Mr Dombey was introduced to Edith Granger who became his second wife, had been visited by Dickens in 1838. There, at Copps's Royal Hotel, they found 'a roaring fire, an elegant dinner, a snug room' awaiting them and, with his usual gratitude, Dickens sent Mr Dombey there. Phiz's drawing of the meeting of the future bride and bridegroom shows a Leamington quite recognizable today; but those pilgrims who may intend to visit it are advised not to do so on a Sunday, when the train-monsters whose speed fascinated Dickens and reminded Dombey of 'the remorseless monster, Death' do *not* proceed with 'a shriek, a roar, and a rattle' towards Leamington; do not proceed at all, in fact, apart from five reluctant trains each way. And, even supposing the traveller reaches Leamington on a Sunday, he may well have the immediate impression that the remorseless monster, Death, has taken the town over for twenty-four hours or so, rendering meals, drinks and amusements impossible of attainment.

The same warning applies to Stratford-on-Avon, visited with perfect ease by Dickens in a post-chaise in 1837. In 1970 it is completely cut off from London by train unless one can find transport from Leamington. Dickens visited Shakespeare's tomb and birthplace, wrote his autograph on the latter's plaster wall (from which his and many other famous names were later erased) and commemorated the tomb in Mrs Nickleby's extraordinary all-night-long dream of 'a black gentleman, at full length, in plaster of Paris, with a lay-down collar tied with two tassels, leaning against a post and thinking'. His visit on the same occasion to Kenilworth and Warwick Castle ('Delightful! Beautiful beyond expression!') found similar immortality in the mouth of 'Cleopatra' Skewton: 'Those darling bygone times, Mr Carker, with their delicious fortresses, and their dear old dungeons, and their delightful places of torture, and their romantic vengeances, and their picturesque assaults and sieges, and everything that makes life truly charming! How dreadfully we have degenerated!'

Dickens, lacking in a sense of, or interest in, history, allowed the party a merely cursory inspection of the treasures Warwick Castle had, and has, to offer. 'Mr Carker, now, having nothing to distract his attention, began to discourse upon the pictures and to select the best, and point them out to Mr Dombey,' but Dickens neither knew nor cared which were the best, nor did he so much as mention the magnificent rooms and furniture, the Murder Room, or Capability Brown's peacock-adorned gardens.

The London scenes of *Dombey and Son*, other than those by the river, are familiar. Walter Gay's first momentous meeting with the lost Florence was in Thames Street (the poor child had wandered there from Good Mrs Brown's lair in Camden Town, a walk almost as incredible for a small girl as Kate Nickleby's daily safari to Wigmore Street). Staggs's Gardens, the home of Polly Toodle and her family, were another reminiscence of Dickens's Bayham Street days, and the City Road, of Micawber associations, was the site of the Charitable Grinders' school to which Polly's son, little 'Biler', was sent.

Where was the church in which Florence and Walter were married? They did not choose St Marylebone, of unhappy memories to them, but a church in the City which has 'a strange smell like a cellar', a shabby little old bell-ringer, and 'an old brown, panelled, dusty vestry'. Perhaps it is that same St Michael's, Queenhithe, where Dickens had sheltered from the rain with Maria Beadnell and talked rapturously of their future marriage, which was never to be. And the sea-beach where old Dombey walks with Florence, her children and the dog Diogenes is surely that of Brighton, where little Paul had asked his sister the question which became enshrined in a popular Victorian ballad:

> *What are the wild waves saying,*
> *Sister, the whole day long?*

The happy marriage of Florence and Walter was not unfortunately a reflection of Dickens's own marital status at the time of the writing of *Dombey and Son*. The house in Devonshire Terrace, a happy home to the Dickens children, was the scene of increasing discontent to their father. Forster suggested that he should write his next book in the first person, a suggestion which he took 'very gravely' and at last accepted, 'though as yet not dreaming of any public use of his early personal trials'. This extremely personal quality in *David Copperfield* was probably the reason why he chose to place David not in his own childhood landscape, Kent, but in a district he had only recently seen for the first time.

In 1848 Dickens, John Leech and Mark Lemon went off on a visit to Norwich and Great Yarmouth. At Norwich he had 'a miserably bad night's rest', from which he hoped to recover by means of the journey coastwards to Yarmouth. The little town fascinated him. 'The strangest place in the world; one hundred and forty-six miles of hill-less marsh between it and London.' Staying at the Royal Hotel, Marine Parade, he planned the locale of the story—his own story, very thinly disguised—which was taking shape in his mind. On the open Denes, near the Nelson monument, was to be the home of Dan'l Peggotty, the 'black barge, or some other kind of superannuated boat . . . high and dry on the ground, with an iron funnel sticking out of it for a chimney and smoking very cosily'. He had seen something of the kind on the marshes of the Thames estuary and been charmed by the idea of living in a boat: could not have been more charmed 'if it had been Aladdin's palace, roc's egg and all'. It was a doll's house for a boy to play with. 'There was a delightful door cut in the side, and it was roofed in, and there were little windows in it; but the wonderful charm of it was, that it was a real boat which had no doubt been upon the water hundreds of times, and which had never been intended to be lived in, on dry land. That was the captivation of it to me,' says David Copperfield, speaking for his creator, and proceeds to describe its humble interior with rapture.

The inn where David met William, the amiable waiter, has been named as either the Duke's Head or the Crown and Anchor.

Legend has it that while staying at Somerleyton Hall, near Lowestoft, with Sir Morton Peto, the civil engineer and railway contractor, Dickens discovered Blundeston. In this village, very slightly rechristened Blunderstone, he gave David Copperfield a birthplace. The Rookery—'David Copperfield all over!' exclaims Betsey Trotwood. 'David Copperfield from head to foot! Calls a house a rookery when there's not a rook near it, and takes the birds on trust because he sees the nests!'—the Rookery into which Miss Trotwood made her devastating entrance on the night of David's birth may have been Blundeston Rectory, from which the church porch and gravestones may be clearly seen, as David describes them. Or it may have been Blundeston Hall, visited by Dickens, which used to have a strange, Cattermole-like appearance, and a view of the church now blotted out by the trees which have grown up. About 1904 the tenant-owner, T. Hardwich Woods, recalled that as a child he was taken by the old housekeeper down the 'long passage . . . leading from Peggotty's kitchen to the front entrance' and shown the 'dark storeroom' opening out of it. The tall old elm-trees, with nests but without rooks, still stood in his garden.

Blundeston Church has a round tower, not the spire of *David Copperfield*, but over the porch there is the sundial which the small David used to see from his window by early light, and think 'Is the sundial glad, I wonder, to be able to tell the time again?'

'Our little village alehouse' from which Barkis started is the Plough Inn, Blundeston, which was indeed the starting-point of the village carrier's round; and in 1848 his name was Barker. His halting-place, half way to Yarmouth, was the small inn at Hopton.

Having thus made a gesture towards concealing autobiography in fiction, Dickens brought David back to London and the actual scenes of his childhood and youth, with only the most perfunctory attempt at disguise. This may have been the reason for his transference of Betsey Trotwood to Dover. The Murdstone and Grinby warehouse was Warren's, moved a little down the river to Blackfriars, and Salem House, the school where David met Steerforth and endured the humiliation of bearing on his back a placard marked 'Take care of him—he bites', was based on Wellington House Academy, just as the sadistic Creakle was based on Mr Jones. He transferred its site to 'down by Blackheath', but from that point the geography of the story sticks pretty closely to fact.

David's terrible journey from London to Dover takes in much of his childhood terrain. It can be followed today, in comfort, by car, taking some two hours from David's 'lodging over the water' near Southwark Bridge. The walk took David six days. The landmarks on his tramp have, in some cases, survived. The Obelisk, where the young man with the donkey-cart robbed him of his box, no longer stands at St George's Circus, but has been moved to a site near 'Old Bedlam', the Imperial War Museum. In the New Kent Road, set in a little garden, one may see a reconstruction of the statue at which David made his first halt: 'a great foolish image in the middle, blowing a dry shell'. Placed there by the Dickens Fellowship, it is in fact a charming, small, infant Triton. Many of the graceful houses ringing Blackheath could stand for Salem House, though one would be unlikely to find a haystack adjacent, as the tired child did and lay down by it. 'Never shall I forget the lonely sensation of first lying down, without a roof over my head!'

Down the 'long dusty track' which was the Dover Road David

continued. The road would take him straight along what is now Shooters Hill Road, part of Watling Street, but modern traffic is diverted to Rochester Way. His road and ours meet again at Rochester, after he has walked 'three-and-twenty miles on the straight road, though not very easily'. Dickens does not dwell on Rochester and Chatham, for they are places of happiness to him, and David is unhappy. Place, to Dickens, is always identifiable with people, a part of the human condition, never objective. The bright landscape rejoices with the joyful man, or mocks his misery; the decaying building reminds him of his own inevitable decay, or comforts his youth with an assurance of its own long endurance and its store of memories. Thus, when David trails into Canterbury after his terrifying adventure with the tinker, his mind is curiously lightened by a vision of his young, dead mother, helping him and leading him on. 'I have associated it, ever since, with the sunny street of Canterbury, dozing as it were in the hot light; and with the sight of its old houses and gateways, and the stately grey Cathedral, with the rooks sailing round the towers. When I came, at last, upon the bare, wide downs near Dover, it relieved the solitary aspect of the scene with hope; and not until I reached that first great aim of my journey, and actually set foot in the town itself . . . did it desert me.'

Canterbury remains associated with happiness for David, as it did for Dickens. (Had, perhaps, some happy dream of Mary Hogarth come to him there, and sanctified the town for ever? Religious images seem to have been identified with her in his mind.) At Canterbury the storm-tossed David finds a haven at the home of Mr Wickfield and his angel-daughter Agnes, David's spiritual 'sister' and better self, who is perhaps a compound of two Hogarth sisters, Mary and Georgina, and an utter opposite to the third, his wife. This is one of the ancient houses which offer security to youth.

'At length we stopped before a very old house bulging out over the road; a house with long low lattice-windows bulging out still farther, and beams with carved heads on the ends bulging out too, so that I fancied the whole house was leaning forward, trying to see who was passing on the narrow pavement below. It was quite spotless in its cleanliness. The old-fashioned brass knocker on the low arched door, ornamented with carved garlands of fruit and flowers, twinkled like a star; the two stone steps descending to the door were as white as if they had been covered with fair linen; and all the angles and corners, and carvings and mouldings, and quaint little panes of glass, and quainter little windows, though as old as the hills, were as pure as any snow that ever fell upon the hills.'

This house has been variously identified. The most favoured candidate, 71 St Dunstan's Street, now the House of Agnes Hotel, does not precisely match the florid description, but Dickens always tends to over-ornament his old buildings, and it will no doubt serve as well as any, a typical example of the beautiful old half-timbered dwellings in which Canterbury was so blessed before the tragic destruction by bombs of so many. Despite the gaping holes made by war, some filled in by modern buildings, despite the not inconsiderable roar of modern traffic, Canterbury retains an extraordinary air of the peace and security Dickens found in it, as did David.

'I loitered through the old streets with a sober pleasure that calmed my spirits and eased my heart . . . the venerable cathedral towers and the old jackdaws and rooks, whose airy voices made them more retired than perfect silence would have done; the battered gateways, once stuck full with statues, long thrown down . . . everywhere, on everything, I felt the same serener air, the same calm, thoughtful, softening spirit.'

It is there in Canterbury today. Perhaps, for once, the objective reached out to Dickens, and matched his own emotion.

The Sun Hotel, in Sun Street by Christchurch Gate, the 'little inn' where Mr Micawber put up and David joined him with Miss Trotwood, Mr Dick and Traddles, is no longer an inn but bears a sign giving its Dickensian connections. Its outward appearance is little changed, for Hitler missed this lovely corner. But the Fountain Hotel in St Margaret's Street, where Dickens himself put up on that occasion when he became a self-appointed guide to the Cathedral, was blitzed. Mr Dick slept there when visiting David at Dr Strong's school, whose exact locale has caused much debate. The visiting Americans to whom Dickens was giving 'pleasant and instructive guidance' on the tour mentioned by George Dolby in *Charles Dickens As I Knew Him* were full of curiosity to see for themselves where David Copperfield went to school: 'There are, however, many houses in Canterbury which would answer to Dickens's description of "Doctor Strong's"; and in reply to one

102

of the party who had asked him to point out the particular house, he said, laughingly, that "there were several that would do".' The King's School, Canterbury, is said by some to have been the place. 'A grave building in a courtyard, with a learned air about it that seemed well suited to the stray rooks and jackdaws who came down from the Cathedral towers to walk with a clerkly bearing on the grass plot.' But Dickens said it was not Dr Strong's, which seems to have been a far more humble establishment than the King's School, which is the most ancient and one of the most famous public schools. The Doctor probably ran one of those Academies for Young Gentlemen which abounded last century. A Georgian house (another bomb casualty) at the corner of Lady Wootton's Green was pointed out as a possible candidate.

The Sun Inn no longer serves such 'beautiful little dinners' as that to which Mrs Micawber entertained David: 'quite an elegant dish of fish; the kidney end of a loin of veal roasted; fried sausage meat; a partridge and a pudding. There was wine, and there was strong ale; and after dinner Mrs Micawber made us a bowl of hot punch with her own hands.' But not the least of twentieth-century Canterbury's virtues is its remarkable choice of restaurants which would have brought a light to the eyes of Dickens, who so loved good food and good cheer, even though the exoticism of some might surprise him.

The grown-up David's lodging at Mrs Crupp's, in chambers ideal for a young gentleman ('and a sweet set this is for sich!'), was the one Dickens himself had occupied as a young reporter, at York House, 15 Buckingham Street, Strand, on the left-hand side near the Water Gate, that beautiful and historic object which Dickens never mentions, although No. 15 overlooked it, and he must have known something of its associations. The house itself was almost equally historic, having at various times had as tenants Bonnie Prince Charlie, Henry Fielding, Peter the Great, and indeed Bacon had been born in the original great York House, of which only the Water Gate remains, but none of this seems to have made any impression on David. He was more concerned about his predecessor in the chambers, who had died of drink and smoke: ' "You don't mean chimneys?" said my aunt. "No, ma'am," returned Mrs Crupp. "Cigars and pipes." ' York House has gone, but the remaining houses on the same side of the little street running from the Strand to the Embankment give a fair idea of its appearance. Near by, half-way down Strand Lane, the Roman Baths, where David (and Dickens) took refreshing cold dips, can still be seen.

Because David's Dora was not Kate, but **Maria Beadnell**, his lost love, he set their honeymoon home in Highgate, where he had dreamed of her so many years before. In *David Copperfield* Highgate, like Canterbury, is a place of idyll, a land where it is always afternoon, despite oysters that won't open and servants who are found in a drunken stupor under the boiler, entertain military deserters in the coal-hole, or go to Greenwich Fair in Dora's bonnet. No shadow here of the realities of Furnival's Inn and Doughty Street. And, because married, adult happiness with Agnes, or Georgina, or anybody, was something his imagination was sadly unable to conceive, Dickens mentioned the home of David and Agnes merely as 'our house in London'. In the last sentence of the book is an unconscious clue, as David apostrophizes Agnes: 'Oh Agnes, Oh my soul, so may thy face be by me when I close my life indeed; so may I, when realities are melting from me like the shadows which I now dismiss, still find thee near me, pointing upward!'

David and Agnes and their marriage have been but shadows; the author is left with his own wretched marriage, and no prospect of its being ended by anything but death.

9

The Last of London

Going down that wide and airy London thoroughfare Southampton Row, from New St Pancras Church with its giant caryatids, one may notice on the wall of the British Medical Association building a tablet to the effect that Charles Dickens once lived in a house on the site. It was Tavistock House, Tavistock Square, and stood in a small, quiet Bloomsbury which knew no monster hotels and towering blocks of flats and offices. The Dickenses moved to it in 1851, when the lease of the Devonshire Terrace house expired. With a family of six sons and two daughters, the eldest boy only fourteen, a bigger home was needed. Dickens bought the lease of Tavistock House from his old friend Frank Stone, A.R.A., and set about getting the place into good order before moving in.

Then, as now, there was more to removal than the mere shifting and arrangement of furniture. Dickens, who described himself as in a state bordering on distraction, 'my new book [*Bleak House*] waiting to be born, and *No Workmen on the Premises*' found that he had to cope with a rat in the kitchen and drains that needed the mysterious process of 'compo-ing', besides structural changes to the rooms. 'Curtains and carpets, on a scale of awful magnitude, are already in preparation, and still—still—No Workmen on the Premises.' Twentieth-century householders may feel for him, wandering up and down the unfinished dwelling, becoming 'low' because the workmen had gone to dinner, tasting glue in the gravy, attended all day long by phantom lime and Irish labourers howling in the schoolroom. Little wonder that he was moved to 'laugh demoniacally'. Significantly, it was he and not Kate who bore the brunt of the worry. She was once more, and for the last time, pregnant.

Tavistock House stood at the north-east corner of Tavistock Square, highly select, behind an iron railing; it, and its neighbours, Russell House and Bedford House, were protected from public invasion by the then respected word 'Private' on both gateposts. Behind the house stretched a large garden, with lawns and high trees, which, said Dickens's visitor Hans Andersen, 'gave a countryfied look in the midst of this coal- and gas-steaming London . . . on the first floor was a rich library, with a fireplace and a writing-table, looking out on the garden . . . the kitchen was underground . . . . I had a snug room looking out on the garden, and over the tree-tops I saw the London towers and spires appear and disappear as the weather cleared or thickened.'

The house contained eighteen rooms, including a drawing-room which would hold over three hundred people, and a schoolroom adapted as a private theatre for those dramatic entertainments in which he delighted, featuring himself, his family and friends. The change which had taken place in Dickens's fortunes may be measured by a glance backwards to the modest little house in Doughty Street. Yet they had been happier then; the entertainments in that great drawing-room, the laughter over the theatricals, had a feverish quality which had not been present when young Dickens had sung 'The Cats'-Meat Man' to a handful of guests and Mary had served the brandy and water.

Tavistock House and its neighbours were demolished in about 1900. In 1880 an eccentric lady, Mrs Georgina Weldon, much given to litigation, published privately an extraordinary pamphlet dealing with *The Ghastly Consequences of Living in Charles Dickens's House*. She failed to make clear quite what it was about Tavistock House that caused these Ghastly Consequences ('the most terrible fate which can befall a human being nowadays— namely that of a sane person shut up in a lunatic asylum, put there for the purpose of being slowly or "accidentally" murdered'), but stated that, although she loved the house dearly, she had suffered there 'days of the most bitter anguish, the most heart-crushing despair', and prefaced her remarks by observing that

106

'Great men . . . have a great deal to answer for'. Mrs Weldon's own state of mind seems to have been, to say the least, unbalanced, but it is permissible to wonder whether the extremes of emotion experienced by Dickens during his residence in the house left some impression upon it. Frustration, anger and violent love have a way of affecting bricks and stone and wood, to those sensitive to such things. Dickens, with his terrifying capacity for passionate feeling, knew all these in the ten years he lived at Tavistock House: in all, they were the unhappiest of his life. 48 Doughty Street is a calm house, 1 Devonshire Terrace was a cheerful one. Perhaps Tavistock House, of all Dickens's homes, was the odd man out and, for once, demolition may have spared subsequent inhabitants from some curious and not altogether pleasant experiences.

Bleak House, the first book written in Tavistock House, was certainly not based on it. According to his description of John Jarndyce's home, it was near St Albans, with a view of the cathedral: 'out of the town, round a corner . . . on the top of a hill before us.' It was at the end of an avenue of trees, up which the carriage drove, and was 'an old-fashioned house, with three peaks in the roof in front, and a circular sweep leading to the porch'. Gombards House, an early Georgian building on the north side of St Albans, has been thought to be the original (though it is in the town, not out of it, by today's measurement) and Great Nast Hyde, off the main St Albans–Hatfield road, has also had supporters. But there is no evidence that he was ever a visitor to either house, or to any particular house in St Albans. He stayed at the Queen's Hotel, Chequer Street, two months after writing the description of Bleak House, and had stayed at the Salisbury Arms, Hatfield, in 1835. The probability is that he made a composite house out of several exteriors.

No such doubts exist about the identity of Chesney Wold, home of Sir Leicester and the tragic Lady Dedlock. In 1849 Dickens stayed at Rockingham Castle, Northamptonshire, with the Hon. Richard Watson and his wife; the first of several happy visits, for there he had a theatre to play with, 'a very elegant little theatre' at that. It was the grandest house Dickens had ever stayed in; not to have used it as a background would have been unthinkable. He admitted to Mrs Watson that 'in some descriptions of Chesney Wold I have taken many bits, chiefly about trees and shadows, from observations made at Rockingham'. A good deal more than trees and shadows, in fact. Chesney Wold is in Lincolnshire, but the description of the landscape surrounding it is that of the flat, watery valley over which Rockingham Castle looms. The Yew Walk of Rockingham is the Ghost's Walk of Chesney Wold; the 'solemn little church' in the park is the one where Esther saw for the first time the face of Lady Dedlock, and in it 'scraps of old remembrances' of her babyhood. In the park woods, looking towards the Ghost's Walk, was the spot where the two women met at last, mother and unacknowledged daughter. The keeper's lodge is there, the sundial, the stable-clock, Mr Tulkinghorn's tower room, the 'pretty house, formerly the parsonage-house', of Mr Boythorn, and the Sondes Arms in the village street is the Dedlock Arms.

Rockingham Castle today is still in the hands of the Watson family. Easily reached from Kettering, Uppingham, Market Harborough or Stamford, it is a good deal more imposing than one might gather from the pages of Dickens, in which, however, the atmosphere and surroundings are wonderfully conveyed; who can forget how 'Solitude, with dusky wings, sits brooding upon Chesney Wold', while the dozing mastiff lies thinking of hot sunshine? But the building itself seems rather an ordinary country house than the royal fortress of reality. Mrs Rouncewell tells a ghost story of the Civil Wars, but omits to mention that all the early kings of England used Rockingham as an armed castle, and that the first Queen Elizabeth granted it to Edward Watson, whose descendants still own it today. Paintings, among which one may fancifully detect Dedlock faces, fine furniture and beautiful Elizabethan gardens invite the visitor with a warmer welcome than the gloomy home in which Mr Guppy and his companions passed from room to room 'raising the pictured Dedlocks for a few brief minutes as the young gardener admits the light, and reconsigning them to their graves as he shuts it out again'. It seems strange that Dickens should thus immortalize a place in which he was to all appearances happy. The conclusion is that he was *not*, in the deepest sense, happy during those holidays at Rockingham, with their house-parties and theatricals.

Bleak House is, on the whole, a gloom-shadowed book, though none the less brilliantly written and impossible to lay aside. Some of the titles he first considered for it convey far more than the one he finally chose: *The Ruined House, Tom-All-Alone's, the Solitary*

House where the Wind howled, The Ruined Mill that got into Chancery and never got out. His characters live under the shadow of Chancery, in and around the hated Inns of Court. He is back with the musty, fusty lawyers' offices of his youth, from the first words of the book: 'London, Michaelmas Term lately over, and the Lord Chancellor sitting in Lincoln's Inn Hall. Implacable November weather . . . smoke, lowering down from chimney-pots . . . fog everywhere . . . and in Lincoln's Inn Hall, at the very heart of the fog, sits the Lord High Chancellor in his High Court of Chancery.'

No longer is Dickens the young reporter making fun of the law. There are no comic Buzfuzes or Snubbinses in *Bleak House.* The decaying buildings symbolize the decay of the human beings destroyed by the Law and the System; *Bleak House* is full of bleak houses. One, in 'a narrow street of high houses, like an oblong cistern to hold the fog' (it was in Thavies Inn), holds Mrs Jellyby, whose life and energies are devoted to African charities, while her baby son cries with his head stuck in the area railings and her neglected young daughter sulks. 'Coavinses' Castle', in nearby Chancery Lane, the sheriff's officer's house where 'poor gentlemen under a cloud' are lodged, is a typically bleak house of the law. In Newman Street, north of Oxford Street, there may still stand the 'dingy' house of Mr Turveydrop, that Model of Deportment, as neglectful of his meek young son as Mrs Jellyby is of her young daughter; among the signs and symbols of the rag trade, what ghostly tinkling of harps and tapping of young ladies' sandals may still emanate from his phantom Dancing Academy?

Mr Snagsby, Law Stationer, 'pursues his lawful calling . . . on the eastern borders of Chancery Lane, that is to say, more particularly in Cook's Court, Cursitor Street. . . . In the shade of Cook's Court, at most times a shady place, Mr Snagsby had dealt in all sorts of blank forms of legal process'. Cook's Court is a thin disguise for Took's Court, still to be found in Cursitor Street. It contains two beautiful early eighteenth-century houses, one of them named Dickens House, and both still keeping a dignified legal air and an appearance of pride in themselves, which suggests that Mrs Snagsby still reigns in one of them. 'She believes the little drawing-room upstairs, always kept, as one might say, with its hair in papers and its pinafore on, to be the most elegant apartment in Christendom.' Below stairs, the lean young woman from a workhouse, possibly christened Augusta but known as Guster, may be getting a dressing-down from Mrs Snagsby, whose temper in girlhood was not improved by a diet of vinegar and lemon-juice.

Standing at his shop door in the dusk, Mr Snagsby could see a late crow skim westward across Chancery Lane and Lincoln's Inn Garden, into Lincoln's Inn Fields. Here was another bleak house, still happily with us: No. 58 Lincoln's Inn Fields . . . 'a large house, a house of state', which had fallen somewhat from its former grandeur, and was let off in suites of rooms. This was, in fact, the house in which John Forster lived; it is a very noble early Georgian mansion, with a Palladian front worthy of the symbolic Roman on the painted ceiling who points downward to the murdered Tulkinghorn. Giacomo Leoni probably built it under the auspices of the enlightened young Earl of Burlington, and the porch was added by Sir John Soane, whose own museum-house is close by. But for Dickens's purposes its pride must be lowered; it becomes the lair of a blackmailer and the scene of his murder.

The grimmest of the bleak houses have gone, fortunately for London. One cannot find today Krook's Rag and Bottle Ware-house, where the rags looked like counsellors' bands and gowns torn up, and the bones in a corner, 'piled together and picked very clean, were the bones of clients', and where Mr Krook suffered the most ghastly death in the pages of Dickens, by Spontaneous Combustion. Upstairs lived old Miss Flite, the mad victim of Chancery, and on the second floor lodged the poor law-writer 'Nemo', Lady Dedlock's ex-lover and father of Esther, whose grave in the little burying-ground gives Dickens the chance of venting his disgust at the overcrowded, insanitary graveyards of London. So scandalously untended were these that even in the graveyard of St Clement Danes bones and skulls protruded from the earth, and a nameless ooze trickled into Fleet Street. The actual place of Nemo's interment, 'a hemmed-in churchyard, pestiferous and obscene, with houses looking in on every side, save where a reek-ing little tunnel of a court gives access to the iron gate', was, on Dickens's own authority, the burial ground for St Mary-le-Strand. He remembered shuddering at it in his boyhood, on those penniless tramps of his round Covent Garden; Phiz's horrible picture shows it as Dickens saw it then, and as it was. In 1853 it was closed, and in 1886 acquired by the Metropolitan Gardens Association, whose task began by clearing away 'heaps of decayed rubbish and the carcases of some eighteen cats'. Now the site is Drury Lane Gardens, where children play and office workers eat their sandwiches.

The bleakest house of all, in the 'black, dilapidated street, avoided by all decent people' and known by the name of Tom-all-Alone's, may have been in any of London's swarming slums. One historian thinks it was part of York Street, Clare Market, Covent Garden, now a respectable, if featureless, area. Dickens took the name from a district of Chatham, and used the place as a symbol of dirt, ignorance and misery, all flourishing beneath the shadow of Chancery.

It is a relief to move from this dark London back to Kent, as it must have been a relief for Dickens himself to take his narrator, Esther, down to Deal to see Richard Carstone at the marine barracks. The darkness follows her at first: 'We came into the narrow streets of Deal, and very gloomy they were, upon a raw misty morning. The long flat beach with its little irregular houses, wooden and brick, and its litter of capstans, and great boats and sheds, and bare upright poles with tackle and blocks, and loose gravelly waste places overgrown with grass and weeds, were as dull an appearance as any place I ever saw.' But, as ever with Dickens himself, the sea and food and drink put a different complexion on the place: 'when we got into a warm room in an excellent hotel . . . Deal began to look more cheerful. Our little room was like a ship's cabin.'

The excellent hotel was the Royal, Deal's principal inn, which had been the Three Kings. Somewhat enlarged, it still opens hospitable doors to the visitor, a place of warmth and welcome where one may enjoy a meal in a dining-room facing the sea, snug from the east coast mist or the breeze blowing off the Goodwins, and at night retire to one of the rooms where Sir William Hamilton stayed, with Emma and Nelson's sister, when Nelson and his fleet lay off Deal in 1801. Possibly the Royal was the 'Admiral Benbow' of Dickens's essay 'Out of Season', from the collection *Reprinted Pieces*.

The marine barracks where poor ineffectual Richard found yet another profession beyond his powers stands composedly behind the built-on site of the old naval yard; strains of military music

111

from the Royal Marines School of Music enliven the air of Deal, that quiet little town by the sea. But the fresh salty air soon gives way to the 'nauseous' atmosphere of Tom-all-Alone's, as Esther, and Dickens, return to London. That 'wind in the East' which gives John Jarndyce an uncomfortable sensation when it blows about Bleak House is an unkind, inland, doom-laden wind.

Rockingham Castle was not the only stately home, with toy theatre thrown in, to be visited by Dickens. In November 1850 there took place at Knebworth, the home of Sir Edward Bulwer-Lytton, what might be called now an amateur drama festival. For three nights in succession a theatrical company headed by Dickens and composed of members of his family and friends performed a double bill: Jonson's comedy *Every Man in his Humour* and the farce *Animal Magnetism*. The performances were in aid of a worthy if somewhat impracticable cause: the Guild of Literature and Art founded by Dickens and 'Bulwer' in aid of impoverished literary men and women. The Guild was a failure, the drama a roaring success.

A relic of such dramatic triumphs survives in one of Dickens's favourite eating-places (and one that is well worth visiting on its own account). Rules Restaurant in Maiden Lane is, ironically enough, only a few yards from the site of the second blacking-factory where the boy Charles suffered the humiliation of working in full public view, and fetched his beer from the public-house opposite. As a middle-aged, immensely successful author, the man Dickens became a patron of Rules. It had been there in his blacking days—had been there, indeed, since 1798. Perhaps he had looked up at its sign, awed, and thought that if he worked hard enough he might be able to dine there when he grew up; perhaps it was a gastronomic Gadshill to him. They are proud to tell you today at Rules how he would go there to write while eating his dinner, or to meet and talk with such friends as Thackeray. The alcove where he sat, in the Edward VII room on the first floor, is named after him, and on a wall in the bar downstairs is one of Rules's treasures, a playbill given to them by Dickens, after another of his double-bill performances. In *Not So Bad As We Seem* Dickens appeared as a Georgian fop, whilst in *Mr Nightingale's Diary* he appeared as six different characters, including an old woman and a sexton. Not in itself a brilliant piece of writing, it was yet historic, for it helped to put into Dickens's mind the idea of impersonating an endless succession of his own characters in dramatic readings.

Sir Edward Bulwer-Lytton, the patron of these dramatic performances, was a man of many parts: statesman, mystic, poet and novelist among them. Romantic, eccentric, he lived in a romantic, eccentric house. Knebworth had been built in 1500 by a Sir Robert Lytton, and had remained a conventional Tudor mansion until Bulwer's mother transformed it into a fantastic place worthy of the pencil of Cattermole. A riot of towers and cupolae, Gothic, pseudo-Tudor and mock-Jacobean, it retained only one feature of its old self—the magnificent banqueting hall, splendid with minstrels' gallery, oak ceiling and screen, and pine panelling attributed to Inigo Jones. It was the perfect setting for a play, particularly a play of the right period. *Every Man in his Humour*, a brilliant Jacobean comedy, gave Dickens the part of a lifetime, that of the swaggering, boastful, cowardly Captain Bobadil, bearded, ruffed and ornately costumed. Typically, Georgina Hogarth played the lead, Mistress Bridget, and 'covered herself with glory', said Dickens, and Kate played nothing at all, for she had sprained her ankle and had to be replaced by the wife of Mark Lemon, who was himself taking part; so were Forster, Douglas Jerrold and John Leech. Dickens threw himself into it all with tremendous energy and enjoyment, producing, acting, arranging with a professionalism worthy of Drury Lane. 'The nights at Knebworth were triumphant!' he exulted afterwards, and it was no idle boast.

The banqueting hall has not changed in essentials since Dickens's day, and is one of the handsomest examples of its kind in the country. The rest of Knebworth has mellowed with time, still fantastic but curiously, almost accidentally, beautiful. It has grown a little, has become a place worth visiting for its relics of Dickens's remarkable friend Bulwer, its portraits and furniture, and a bed in which Queen Elizabeth I is reputed to have slept—correctly, perhaps, for once, for she visited Knebworth in 1588. The little Hertfordshire village and the countryside around are charming.

Dickens visited the house again in 1861 and 1865. He was gratified by the sight of the Guild Houses, built for those indigent characters on whose behalf the Knebworth performances had raised funds: a block of three houses in appropriately Gothic style near the Stevenage road. After inspecting the dwellings,

Dickens, Bulwer and a party of members of the Guild drove to Knebworth to enjoy Bulwer's hospitality, and Dickens made a brief but striking speech. 'Life is short, and why should speeches be long?' he quoted, and went on to say that he would adopt this aphorism, 'particularly in the circumstances in which we are placed, with this delicious weather and such charming gardens near us'. He praised Bulwer for his gift of the land in which the houses were built, proposed his health, and promised the occupants of the houses that they would never be looked down upon for living there, and would be 'invited to occupy them as artists, receiving them as a mark of the high respect in which they are held by their fellow-workers'.

Alas for idealism, his promises were not taken seriously. Nobody came to occupy the Guild Houses, which were regarded as too far from London in the first place, and little better than alms-houses in the second. After remaining empty for nearly twenty years they were converted into villas. Opposite them, an inn was later renamed *Our Mutual Friend*.

The 1861 visit took place just after Dickens had finished *Great Expectations*: he needed a little holiday in Hertfordshire, one of his favourite counties. With Arthur (later Sir Arthur) Helps, once the Queen's Secretary, he called upon a local eccentric known as Mad Lucas, at Elmwood House near Stevenage. This curious character was supposed to have gone mad after the death of his mother, whose corpse he refused to bury, to the embarrassment of the local authorities. He lived in bare, unfurnished rooms, wore instead of clothes a loose blanket fastened with a skewer, and took his meals among piles of cinders and rubbish in the kitchen; sharing them, very generously, with the rats. His stock diet consisted of bread and cheese, red herrings, and gin, but he kept fine wines in the house for visitors, with a particularly good sherry for ladies.

It was not in Dickens to pass by such rich material. Mad Lucas appeared, quite recognizably, under the name of Mopes, in the sketch 'Tom Tiddler's Ground' (*All the Year Round*, Christmas 1861, republished in an abbreviated form in *Christmas Stories*). The district is similarly recognizable: 'a nook in a rustic by-road ... down among the pleasant dales and trout-streams of a green English county. No matter what county. Enough that you may hunt there, shoot there, fish there, traverse long grass-grown

114

Roman roads there, open ancient barrows there, see many a square mile of richly cultivated land there, and hold Arcadian talk with a bold peasantry, their country's pride, who will tell you (if you want to know) how pastoral housekeeping is done on nine shillings a week.' The clue to Stevenage is given by the reference to ancient barrows—the tumuli called the Six Hills, supposed to be Danish burial-places. The inn which Dickens calls the Peal of Bells is the White Hart, where Dickens and Helps called to ask the way to Lucas's house. Lucas is said to have denied that Dickens ever visited him, but the conversation between Mopes and the fastidious Traveller has an authentic ring: '"You are an insolent person! Go away from my premises. Go!" said the Hermit in an imperious and angry tone. "Come, come!" returned Mr Traveller, quite undisturbed. "This is a little too much. You are not going to call yourself clean? Look at your legs."'

Elmwood House, indescribably filthy, was pulled down in 1893, nineteen years after the hermit's death.*

Bleak House was followed in 1854 by *Hard Times*. Of all Dickens's novels it is the one in which place has the least personality. He deals in it with the evils of unimaginative, soulless education exemplified by the hard-headed Gradgrind, the miseries of the factory hand Stephen Blackpool, caught up in an imperfect industrial system and unable to divorce his drunken wife, and the victimization of Gradgrind's daughter, Louisa, forced into a loveless marriage. The setting is 'Coketown', generally supposed to be Manchester. He had visited it in 1838, 1843, 1847 and again in 1852. In 1841 his sister Fanny maried Henry Burnett, an operatic singer who taught music in Manchester after leaving the stage; Fanny, herself a trained musician, helped him in the training of the choir at Rusholme Road Congregational Chapel. The Burnetts lived in one of the dignified Georgian houses in Upper Brook Street, behind Oxford Road (now fallen on evil days), where Dickens probably visited them; their crippled son was the original of Tiny Tim and Paul Dombey. In 1838 Dickens was certainly a guest of Gilbert Winter at Stocks House, Cheetham Hill Road, a moated mansion which was probably the manor-house of Cheetham Manor; here he met those philanthropic Quakers, the

* A full and interesting account of all that is known about Lucas is given in *Highways and Byways in Hertfordshire*, by Frederick L. Griggs (Macmillan, 1902).

brothers William and Daniel Grant, who lived at Springside, Ramsbottom, 'which they made a veritable home of hospitality and good works'. They emerged in the next year (1839) as the Cheeryble brothers of *Nicholas Nickleby*. Stocks House was pulled down in 1884.

Dickens's diary for 1838 records, on his return from Manchester to London, 'Chaise to Cheadle, £1.1.0 . . . Bill at Inn, £4.0.0.' The inn is said to be the George and Dragon, one of the two coaching inns of the little Cheshire village. Clearly, he knew Manchester and its environs well, but the description of Coketown does not seem to fit it very closely. 'It was a town of red brick, or of brick that would have been red if the smoke and ashes had allowed it . . . a town of machinery and tall chimneys, out of which interminable serpents of smoke trailed themselves for ever and ever, and never got uncoiled. It had a black canal in it, and a river that ran purple with ill-smelling dye.' This last might certainly be the Manchester Ship Canal and the Irwell (one of the present authors recalls it running with dye of a great many colours through an unblitzed Manchester). The library mentioned could be the Athenaeum. But otherwise Coketown is a fairly insignificant place. Manchester had, in Dickens's lifetime, several distinctive buildings: the Cathedral, known as T'Owd Church, the lovely Chetham's Hospital, nests of charming half-timbered houses in the Old Shambles, and at least one inn humming with history, the Seven Stars, said to have been a hatching-place for the Gunpowder Plot. The Georgian infirmary and its grounds were a pleasant open space in the centre of Piccadilly. Streets now completely commercialized were largely residential; the Grants had houses in Mosley Street and Cannon Street. Deansgate, where Dickens appeared with his theatrical company and later gave readings at the Free Trade Hall, was then full of graceful houses, as was (and is still) the St Ann's Square district. Only just outside the city were the pleasant suburbs of Rusholme, handsome Platt Hall in its park, rural Fallowfield and Didsbury. None of this seems to equate with a town which 'contained several large streets all very like one another, and many small streets still more like one another'.

Perhaps he meant Preston. He stayed at the Bull Hotel there in 1854, and found the town 'a nasty place', while the Bull was dismissed as 'an old, grubby, smoky, mean, intensely formal red-brick

116

house'.* One suspects that he had had a bad dinner there, as he probably had at the Great White Horse of Ipswich. There is something distinctly liverish about the description of Coketown. He denied that it was Preston, yet it was only politic to do so, for he had stayed there during a strike, and the strike leader, Mortimer Grimshaw, saw himself as the original of the odious Slackbridge of *Hard Times* and protested.

It is impossible to say where one might find either Stone Lodge, the Gradgrind home in 'the outskirts of the city, which was neither town nor country, and yet was either spoiled', or the Pegasus's Arms in Pod's End, of which the only feature worth remembering is the theatrical tinsel which Gradgrind and Bounderby saw framed and glazed behind the bar, of a stage Pegasus 'with real gauze let in for his wings, golden stars stuck on all over him, and his ethereal harness made of red silk'. It is one of the rare flashes of the young Dickens which all too seldom illuminate *Hard Times*. Because he was preaching, not feeling, the places of the story are no more real or alive than its characters, no more convincing than the dreadful parody of Lancashire dialect spoken by Stephen Blackpool and his kind.

'How I work, how I walk, how I shut myself up, how I roll down hills and climb up cliffs; how the new story is everywhere, heaving in the sea, flying with the clouds, blowing in the wind; how I settle to nothing and wonder (in the old way) at my own incomprehensibility.' Dickens was writing from the Pavilion Hotel, Folkestone, a modest, newish building on the front, later to be enlarged and transformed, as was Folkestone itself. Then the town was small, quiet, a jumping-off point for the Continent and a survival of smuggling days. It was the kind of town Dickens liked, especially at this time in his life when London was more than ever a place of darkness and despair to him. 'The little old fishing and smuggling town remains . . . there are break-neck flights of ragged steps, connecting the principal streets by backways, which will cripple the visitor in half an hour. . . .' Much of Dickens's Folkestone remains today, steep cobbled streets, the harbour district where one can buy shellfish from stalls (an increasingly rare experience in a seaside town), the area round the parish church. Even

---

* Although he may have relented towards it in 1868: see page 150.

117

the newer part, the Leas and their big hotels and the wide shopping streets, have a Victorian air which he would recognize. In *Household Words* he called the place Pavilionstone, writing of it rhapsodically and at length, for it was giving him a blessed pause from his troubles. He liked both the old and the new Folkestone. 'The South Eastern Company have brought Pavilionstone into such vogue with their tidal trains and splendid steam packets, that a new Pavilionstone is rising up. I am, myself, of New Pavilionstone. We are a little mortary and limey at present, but we are getting on capitally . . . we are sensibly laid out in general; and with a little care and pains (by no means wanting, so far) shall become a very pretty place. We ought to be, for our situation is delightful, our air is delicious, and our breezy hills and downs, carpeted with wild thyme, and decorated with millions of wild flowers, are, on the faith of a pedestrian, perfect.'

He had no regrets for the old coaching days, when he contemplated the Great Pavilionstone Hotel: 'A thoroughly good inn, in the days of coaching and posting, was a noble place. But no such inn would have been equal to the reception of four or five hundred people, all of them wet through, and half of them dead sick,* every day in the year . . . everything is done for you; every service is provided at a fixed and reasonable charge; all the prices are hung up in all the rooms, and you can make out your own bill beforehand, as well as the book-keeper. . . .'

The noise of itinerant musicians had finally driven him from Broadstairs. He had tried the Isle of Wight for a change, in 1849, renting a villa at Bonchurch, but found the climate 'too relaxing' for himself and the family. Folkestone seemed to be the answer to his needs, and in the summer of 1855 he rented 3 Albion Villas and moved his family down for a long holiday in this 'very pleasant little house overlooking the sea', which stands today (though considerably uglified) and bears a plaque commemorating his residence in it, placed there by the Dickens Fellowship.

The 'new story' which was in the sea, in the clouds, in the wind, ruling his mind, was *Little Dorrit*. With the extraordinary detachment of which he was capable, he sat on bright September mornings at his desk by an open window, with 'the sky and ocean framed before me like a beautiful picture', and wrote of London at its

* After the Channel crossing.

darkest and most sinister. Arthur Clennam, his hero who is not a hero but a haunted man like himself, arrives from Marseilles to find an unpleasant welcome awaiting him. Sitting in a coffee-house on Ludgate Hill on a Sunday evening, 'gloomy, close and stale', he reflects on the miseries of the English Sabbath, and Dickens works off a sharp indictment of that institution: 'Maddening church bells of all degrees of dissonance . . . throbbing, jerking, tolling, as if the Plague were in the city and the dead-carts were going round. Everything was bolted and barred that could by possibility furnish relief to an over-worked people . . . nothing to change the brooding mind, or raise it up. . . .'

The very streets could certainly have done with a little enlivenment, Arthur felt: 'Fifty thousand lairs surrounded him where people lived so unwholesomely, that fair water put into their crowded rooms on Saturday night, would be corrupt on Sunday morning; albeit my lord, their county member, was amazed that they failed to sleep in company with their butcher's meat. Miles of close wells and pits of houses, where the inhabitants gasped for air, stretched far away towards every point of the compass. Through the heart of the town a deadly sewer ebbed and flowed, in the place of a fine fresh river.'

Dickens's personal fiends were not altogether responsible for this sickened outburst. Since his young days London had changed, as well as he; had outgrown its housing capacity without the benefit of a proper drainage system. The Thames was literally, as he said, a sewer. Parliamentary debates in warm weather were almost unendurable because of it, the consequences to public health incalculable. Six years after *Little Dorrit* was written, the Prince Consort died of typhoid fever: his was only one such death among hundreds and thousands unrecorded.

Arthur Clennam's homecoming was no more cheerful, to the dingy old brick house behind rusty railings, propped up on 'some half-dozen or so gigantic crutches'. We are not told where the house was, but the situation and description suggest that it may have been the one in Thames Street where Mrs Nickleby and Kate had lodged so uncomfortably. To write of its final, symbolic collapse must have given Dickens great satisfaction.

The hub of the book is the Marshalsea. Once again we are in the place of Dickens's childhood miseries. Arthur Clennam, when visiting it for the first time, reflected that 'it was as haggard a view of life as a man need look upon'. Harsh, photographic reality characterizes this Marshalsea. The incidents of his childhood are recapitulated without much disguise: his father is Old Dorrit (there had been a Dorrett in the prison at the time of John Dickens's incarceration); Little Dorrit, the child born and reared in prison, is his own innocent self transformed into a girl with a dash of Mary Hogarth. She has a sister who is called Fanny and becomes a dancer; she is not very like Fanny Dickens, but the clues are there.

Two architectural monuments remain to the book and its heroine: the Marshalsea walls and St George's Church, Borough, across Angel Place from the garden once its graveyard. It is and always will be 'Little Dorrit's Church' to Dickensians sweeping by on their way to or from Kent. Here she was christened, crouched on the steps with the poor creature Maggy after being shut out from the Marshalsea, and by permission of the verger spent the night in the vestry, with her head on 'that sealed book of Fate', the burial register; and here, at last, she was married to Arthur Clennam. Her memorial is a small prayerful figure in a modern window at the east end of the church.

The rest of London, as it unrolls like a grimy map, is familiar. The proud Merdles live in Dombey country, at the handsomest house in Harley Street. Old Mr Casby and the gushing Flora Finching, a cruel caricature of the middle-aged Maria Beadnell, live somewhere off Gray's Inn Road. Arthur Clennam lodges in Covent Garden; Pancks and Rugg in Mr Brownlow's Pentonville; Dorrit's solicitors, Peddle and Pool, are surely not far from the abode of Mrs Todgers at their offices in Monument Yard. 'Mr. F.', Flora's late husband, had been educated at a school in Blackheath: Salem House, no doubt. And, not unlike David Copperfield, though in a less literal sense, Mr Dorrit was 'waylaid at Dartford, pillaged at Gravesend, rifled at Rochester, fleeced at Sittingbourne, and sacked at Canterbury'. Well may Mr F.'s Aunt, that trenchant Sibyl, remark that: 'There's milestones on the Dover Road.' Milestones indeed they were, in the life of her creator.

The year 1859 was a year of crisis and decision for Dickens. On 29th April he gave the first of those public readings, for his own benefit, which had had their inception on a charity reading at Birmingham in 1853; another had followed at Folkestone in 1855. In May, Kate Dickens left Tavistock House for ever. Husband and wife were finally separated in fact as they had been for years in sympathy. Nothing, Dickens told Forster, could put things right 'until we are all dead and buried and risen'. Kate and her eldest son, Charley, went off to live in a house in Gloucester Terrace, Regent's Park. Dickens, left in Bloomsbury with his other children and Georgina for housekeeper, was 'like a madman', said his daughter Katey. He was in love with a young actress, Ellen Ternan, but could not, would not, admit it. He had foolishly published a refutation of gossip which had only added fuel to the fire and had quarrelled with his publishers, Bradbury and Evans. Action being his only lifeline, he flung himself into the publication of the weekly journal *All the Year Round*, successor to *Household Words*. 'The Chief', as his awed staff called him, was seen daily on his brisk way to his office at 26 Wellington Street, Strand, at the corner of Exeter Street, almost opposite the Lyceum Theatre.* He was no longer the inspired young angel of Maclise's portrait, but a bearded, lined, grizzled man, whose still brilliant eyes looked out at the world with a kind of defiance beneath beetling brows.

Four years previously, in March 1855, he had taken a step which was to change the last decade of his life. 'This day,' he wrote to Forster on 14th March, 'I have paid the purchase money for Gadshill Place.'

* now replaced by commercial buildings.

10

Gadshill

It was the house of his dream: the dream of happy childhood. In *The Uncommercial Traveller* he tells the story, so often repeated by biographers, of how, as 'a very queer small boy . . . not more than half as old as nine', he was often taken by his father as a treat to see a house on a hill, half way between Rochester and Gravesend. When he was nine he would go by himself to look at it. 'And ever since I can recollect, my father, seeing me so fond of it, has often said to me "If you were to be very persevering and were to work hard, you might some day come to live in it."'

Not only the hard work which was his anodyne, but one of those curious chances in which he took delight ('few things moved his fancy so pleasantly'), brought about his long-cherished ambition. Passing it one day in the course of a country walk with his *Household Words* colleague W. H. Wills, he told Wills the story of his early admiration for the house. That evening, Wills 'took down to dinner' Mrs Lynn Linton, novelist and journalist. The conversation turned on the district which Wills had just left, and Mrs Lynn Linton talked of it knowledgeably. 'You know it?' asked Wills. 'Oh, yes,' she said, 'I know it very well. I was a child there in the house they call Gadshill Place. My father was the Rector, and lived there many years. He has just died, left it to me, and I want to sell it.'

So at last the house which had haunted him for thirty-five years came to Charles Dickens. Its ghost had appeared at least once, in

122

the most ghostly of his books. Scrooge, led back to his boyhood, had returned to his old school: 'a mansion of dull red brick, with a little weathercock-surmounted cupola, on the roof, and a bell hanging in it.' This is a swift sketch of the exterior of Gadshill Place. Inside was 'a long bare melancholy room, made barer still by lines of plain deal forms and desks. At one of these a lonely boy was reading near a feeble fire; and Scrooge sat down upon a form, and wept to see his poor forgotten self as he used to be'.

It would delight Dickens to know that a century after his death, Gadshill Place would be indeed a school, and that two of his own great-great-granddaughters would be educated there.

His ardent admirer, young Percy Fitzgerald, was dazzled by his first visit to his hero's new possession. 'Mystic enchantment . . . one of the prettiest, most entrancing pictures of a literary man's domestic life—golden and glittering and almost fascinating. Gadshill is a *riant*, cheerful house. Its effect is almost dramatic. The windows and their disposition have a character; so has the roof, with its piquant cupola. No one could pass it without being attracted by it. The back, also, has character of its own. . . . It always seemed to me a pleasant-looking, picturesque house, with a comfortable, glowing, even rubicund air.' It was in fact a plainish square-faced house of red brick, built about 1779 (not, as the architecturally vague Dickens thought, in the reign of George I), with a handsome portico and some fine cedars in the garden which belonged to it across the Dover Road, in the 'shrubbery'. This, and twenty years' lease of a meadow at the end of the back garden, went with the house.

Having bought the house and satisfied his ambition, Dickens immediately lost interest in it. 'He had no thought at this time of reserving the place wholly for himself, or of making it his own residence except at intervals of summer', says Forster. 'He looked upon it as an investment only.' It was to replace Fort House, Broadstairs, as a holiday home for himself, Georgina and the family. The only way in which he could revive his waning enthusiasm was by launching into a heavy programme of improvements to the place. He built on a new drawing-room and two new bedrooms, transformed another bedroom into a study and a breakfast-room into a 'retreat fitted up for smokers' (those banes of Victorian womanhood) with a billiard-table in it. The hall acquired a fashionable parquet floor and a new staircase, an ancient coach-house was replaced by 'a capital servants' hall' and the loft above it by a schoolroom for his sons. Out of a waste piece of orchard he made a croquet-lawn. A passage was constructed under the road connecting the front garden with the 'shrubbery'; no mere functional thing, but a romantic tunnel with a classical mask over the garden entrance. A conservatory arose, fulfilment of another of Dickens's dreams: 'glass and iron, brilliant but expensive, with foundations as of an ancient Roman work of horrible solidity.' There was no water laid on, so a well had to be put in (a process 'like putting Oxford Street endwise, and laying gas along it'). 'We are still boring for water here,' he told Forster in July 1856, 'at the rate of two pounds per day for wages. The men seem to like it very much, and to be perfectly comfortable.'

There were snags, of course, which all added to the excitement the new householder craved. 'The horse has gone lame from a sprain, the big dog has run a tenpenny nail into one of his hind feet, the bolts have all flown out of the basket-carriage, and the gardener says all the fruit trees want replacing with new ones . . . five men have been looking attentively at the pump for a week, and (I should hope) may begin to fit it in the course of October.' As with Tavistock House, he found the carpenters 'absolutely maddening. They are always at work yet never seem to do anything'.

All these alterations took years to complete. At first he remained detached from them, writing to Forster in January 1858: 'You will hardly know Gadshill again, I am improving it so much—yet I have no interest in the place.' But the lust for house-converting, which is like no other lust, seized him and carried him along with it—'just the kind of occasional occupation and resource his life most wanted in its next seven or eight years', says Forster. His daughter Mamie said after his death that 'he was full of the kind of interest in the house which is commonly confined to women'. It was, also, an expression of his reforming zeal. He did to Gadshill what he would have liked to do to the world, cleaning, repairing, replacing the old with the new, ventilating and enlarging and letting light into dark places.

'My little Kentish freehold' became the joy of his life, with its view as pretty as one might find in a long day's ride and its convenient situation. Cobham Woods and Park, behind, offered wonderful scope for those long walks which were a necessity to

29

St George's Church, Southwark, where Little Dorrit was married.

Gadshill Place, Kent, the house of Dickens's youthful fancy which became his last home.

Joe Gargery's cottage, in Great Expectations, *at Chalk, near Gravesend, Kent. Joe's forge adjoins it.*

31
32

The thirteen graves of children of the Comport family in Cooling churchyard, near Gravesend, Kent: in Great Expectations *the graves of Pip's brothers and sisters.*

34

The Swiss chalet given to Dickens by Fechter, the actor. It stood in the grounds of Gadshill and is now in the garden of Eastgate House, Rochester, part of which is a Dickens museum. Dickens was writing Edwin Drood *in the upper room immediately before his death.*

◁ *Restoration House, Rochester, Kent. In* Great Expectations *it is Miss Havisham's home, Satis House.*

The Watts
Memorial,
Rochester
Cathedral,
Kent ('The
Seven Poor
Travellers').
The tomb
below is that
of Dean Hole
(The Mystery
of Edwin
Drood).

35

36

CHARLES DICKENS
DID NOT
LIVE HERE

Emphatic
disclaimer by
a resident of
Broadstairs,
Kent.

The Leather Bottle, Cobham, Kent, Dickens's 'local' during the Gadshill years, but used by him long before in The Pickwick Papers.

38

John Jasper's Gatehouse, Rochester, Kent, and the cathedral (The Mystery of Edwin Drood).

him; beloved Rochester and Chatham were only a little way down the road, and the Railway had come to Rochester, connecting it with the coast and France, to which he liked to make frequent excursions. Besides, it had the amusing distinction of being built where Falstaff and his mates robbed the travellers, 'and Falstaff ran away from the identical spot of ground now covered by the room in which I write. A little rustic alehouse, called the Sir John Falstaff, is over the way, has been over the way ever since, in honour of the event.'

In the autumn of 1860 he sold Tavistock House and transferred the contents to Gadshill. He was never again to live in London except in temporary lodgings and his rooms at the Wellington Street offices. Gadshill became the background to one who had been a reluctant townsman, drawn to busy streets by the life in them, but who craved open space in which to work off his fantastic energies, and a place in which to entertain a literally endless series of friends. For he could not bear to be alone. In London friends had come to dinner, then left him with only his family about him. At Gadshill he found both freedom and stimulus.

In June 1859, just over a year after his separation from Catherine, Dickens moved himself and the family to Gadshill for the summer, with a week at Broadstairs to round it off. His new novel, *A Tale of Two Cities*, was finished. He first historical novel since *Barnaby Rudge*, it was a powerful, dramatic story of the French Revolution. It begins in Kent: not the Kent of Gadshill, but the Dover Road, where it climbs Shooter's Hill to emerge on Blackheath. The heavy mail-coach struggles up the muddy road, somewhere below the Coach and Horses Inn, apparently. It is bound for the Royal George Hotel, Dover. This, almost certainly, was the Ship, where Dickens had stayed in 1856, and which Byron had celebrated in verse:

> *Thy cliffs, dear Dover! harbour and hotel;*
> *Thy custom-house, with all its delicate duties;*
> *Thy waiters running mucks at every bell;*
> *Thy packets, all whose passengers are booties*
> *To those who upon land and water dwell;*
> *And last, not least, to strangers uninstructed,*
> *Thy long, long bills, whence nothing is deducted.*

Next time Dickens visited the Ship it had been rebuilt as the Lord

Warden Hotel. It was a victim of the Second World War, and has now been rebuilt once more with the architectural incongruity shared by the enormous blocks of flats which loom clumsily over Dover harbour, coarse giants beside the dainty little Regency houses which were spared at the northern tip of the crescent. But Dickens liked it in its earlier version, writing in 1863 of the charms of Dover as seen from the Calais packet.

'Mr and Mrs Birmingham, host and hostess of the Lord Warden Hotel, are my much esteemed friends, but they are too conceited about the comforts of that establishment when the Night Mail is starting. I know it is a good house to stay at, and I don't want the fact insisted upon in all its warm bright windows at such an hour. I know the Warden is a stationary edifice that never rolls or pitches, and I object to its big outline seeming to insist upon that circumstance, and, as it were, to come over me with it, when I am reeling on the deck of that boat. . . . As I wait here on the night packet, for the South Eastern Train to come down with the Mail, Dover appears to me to be illuminated for some intensely aggravating festivity in my personal dishonour. All its noises smack of taunting praises of the land, and dispraises of the gloomy sea, and of me for going on it.'

The Dover of *A Tale of Two Cities* is in 1775 what it was until bombing devastated it: a 'little, narrow, crooked town' hiding away from the invading sea, its air 'of so strong a piscatory flavour that one might have supposed sick fish went up to be dipped in it, as sick people went down to be dipped in the sea'. What remains of that old town is disappearing day by day, the narrow alleys with their shuttered shops, the cottages climbing up the hilly streets to the heights that are riddled with tunnel and cave, dotted with ghostly fortifications. The air is no longer fishy, the Channel passage is no more a dramatic and dangerous undertaking.

London, one of the Two Cities of the book, is, like Dover, a place of the eighteenth century. Hanging Sword Alley, ('Mr Cruncher's apartments were not in a savoury neighbourhood'), is now (and was in Dickens's time) among the great newspaper buildings, 'given up to printing machines', as William Kent observed. Sydney Carton would have had to fight his way through pressmen to draw Charles Darnay into the little room where Darnay was soon 'recruiting his strength with a good plain dinner and good wine', for it was, Dickensians believe, the Cheshire

Cheese, frequented by customers literary and legal, and by Dickens himself. It would be instructive to hear Dickens's comments on today's lunch-time beer sessions at the Cheese and its Fleet Street neighbours. 'Those were drinking days, and most men drank hard,' he says of the meetings of Stryver and Carton at the Cheese. 'What the two drank together, between Hilary Term and Michaelmas, might have floated a king's ship.'

The site of Dr Manette's London house has been a matter of keen controversy for players of the Dickens Geography Game.* Robert Allbut asserted that Carlisle House, at the end of Carlisle Street, Soho Square, was the right house. William Kent thought it was 10 Manette Street, between Charing Cross Road and Beak Street (it was Rose Street in Dickens's time), where a large, dignified eighteenth-century house, now called Artists' House and owned by Foyle's, is pointed out as possibly having been the home of Doctor Manette and Lucie. 'A quainter corner than the corner where the Doctor lived, was not to be found in London. There was no way through it, and the front windows of the Doctor's lodgings commanded a pleasant little vista of street that had a congenial air of retirement on it. There were few buildings then, north of the Oxford-road, and forest-trees flourished, and wild flowers grew, and the hawthorn blossomed, in the now vanished fields'. Tradition goes that here, 'in a building at the back, attainable by a courtyard where a plane-tree rustled its green leaves, church-organs claimed to be made, and silver to be chased, and likewise gold to be beaten by some mysterious giant who had a golden arm starting out of the wall of the front hall—as if he had beaten himself precious, and menaced a similar conversion of all visitors'. This same tradesman's sign now starts out of the staircase wall at 48 Doughty Street.

While he was writing *A Tale of Two Cities* Dickens had not yet fully succumbed to the lure of Gadshill. In his papers for *All the Year Round*,† written between 1859 and 1861, scenes of his childhood constantly reappear: Chatham, Rochester, the Gadshill district, even Camden Town. Slowly, the house was taking him over. He says of it in his essay 'Tramps' in *The Uncommercial*

---

* There is an interesting paper on Dr Manette's house in *The Dickensian* for August, 1905.

† *The Haunted House, The Uncommercial Traveller*, etc.

Traveller that 'all the tramps with carts or caravans—the Gipsy-tramp, the Show-tramp, the Cheap Jack—find it impossible to resist the temptations of the place', of that 'piece of Kentish Road . . . high and airy, with a distant river stealing steadily away to the ocean, like a man's life'.

While writing one of these pieces he was suddenly struck by 'a very fine, new and grotesque idea'. This was the germ of *Great Expectations*, in which he again returned to the 'I' of *David Copperfield*, was again a boy facing hard trials in an adult world. Young Pip gains wealth, but loses his heart to the cold beauty Estella. Biographers have seen in his situation a parallel to that of Dickens at the time, desperately wooing the tormenting Ellen Ternan, just as they have seen a reflection of Ellen in the blonde Lucie Manette, 'the golden-haired doll'. We do not, and never shall, know with any certainty Dickens's intimate history at this time, but that he felt deeply, was full of an emotion transcending plot, and was in his own mind identified with Pip, is unmistakable. Significantly, he sets the story in the district closest to his heart, where he has after so many years again taken root.

'Ours was the marsh country, down by the river, within, as the river wound, twenty miles of the sea.' The Hundred of Hoo, lying to the east of the Dover Road, was Dickens's view from the windows of Gadshill. It had a different look from the surrounding countryside; one of those ancient, bleak, mysterious peninsulas, a misty relief-map leading the eye to the Isle of Grain. Forster remembered how Dickens planned the opening of the book: 'It is strange, as I transcribe the words, with what wonderful vividness they bring back the very spot on which we stood when he said he meant to make it the scene of the opening of his story—Cooling Castle ruins and the desolate church, lying out among the marshes seven miles from Gadshill.' Pip, telling his own tale, says that 'my first most vivid and broad impression of the identity of things, seems to me to have been gained on a memorable raw afternoon towards evening. At such a time I found out for certain, that this bleak place overgrown with nettles was the churchyard; and that Philip Pirrip, late of this parish, and also Georgiana wife of the above, were dead and buried, and that Alexander, Bartholomew, Abraham, Tobias, and Roger, infant children of the aforesaid, were also dead and buried, and that the dark flat wilderness beyond the churchyard, intersected with dykes and mounds and gates, with scattered cattle feeding on it, was the marshes; and that the low, leaden line beyond was the river; and that the distant savage lair from which the wind was rushing, was the sea.'

Cooling today is more populous than in 1860. But Dickens would have no doubt where he was, from the first glimpse of the imposing towers of Cooling's ruined medieval moated castle, with its proud assertion on a copper plate whose original was fixed there 600 years ago:

> *Knoweth that beth and schul be,*
> *That i am mad in helpe of the Cuntree.*
> *In knowing of whyche thyng*
> *Thys is chartre and wytnessing.*

It was built in 1387 to aid Kent against the menace of France; but its only attacker was an Englishman, Sir Thomas Wyatt, who besieged it in 1554 during his rebellion against Mary I. Sir John Oldcastle, Lord Cobham, lived there, the innocent original of Falstaff: 'Oldcastle died a martyr, and this is not the man.' Dickens does not seem to have followed up the connection with the legendary rogue who ran away on the spot covered by his study, though in his wildly prejudiced *Child's History of England* he refers to Henry the Fifth's sacrifice of his friend to the priests who represented Cobham's Lollardry as treason. 'It is much easier to burn men than to burn their opinions . . . he was carried to London in a horse-litter, was fastened by an iron chain to a gibbet, and so roasted to death.'

Within the ruins of the castle is a farmhouse, owned in Dickens's time by a farmer called Murton, where in the latter half of the eighteenth century lived a branch of the Comport family. Whether ill-luck or the then prevalent marsh fever beset them we do not know, but they were the parents of seven of the infants whose little tombstones in Cooling churchyard gave Dickens the idea of making Pip the sole survivor of a family of six brothers. He mentions only five stones, but in fact there are thirteen. The seven children of Michael and Jane Comport were Mary, three Williams, a James, Frances and Elizabeth, all dead before their second year. Mary died in 1767, her sister Elizabeth, the last of the children, in 1799. For eighteen years the poor mother produced baby after baby, only to see each one carried to the lonely churchyard. The children she managed to rear had no better luck with their offspring: the other infants beneath the lozenge-shaped stones are all Comport descendants, and in the churchyards of High Halstow and All Hallows are yet more. Of all the sad little stones, not one has a legible inscription. One only bears a faintly decipherable name, John. He was the youngest of all, 'John Rose Baker, died June 9, 1837, aged one month'.

Characteristic of the extraordinary chiaroscuro of Dickens's nature is a story of him told by his American friend, the publisher J. T. Fields. While on a visit to Gadshill in 1869 he and a party of friends were taken by Dickens to see the little tombs at Cooling. Perhaps they expected some gentle reflections on infant mortality from the man who had written so tenderly of the deaths of children. Instead, their unpredictable host chose a good flat gravestone, laid a napkin on it, spread out the contents of the well-filled picnic hampers, and proceeded to impersonate, 'with fantastic eagerness', a first-class head waiter.

It has often been assumed that Joe Gargery's forge and the cottage where Pip was 'brought up by hand' by his neurotic sister * was at Cooling, because of the identification of the churchyard in the first chapter of the book, and of Dickens's admission to Forster. But he may have performed his usual trick of mixing up localities to suit himself; perhaps, in this case, because of the annoying tendency of people to identify themselves with his fictitious characters. He had had trouble over such cases as his cartoon of Leigh Hunt as Harold Skimpole. There may have been strong personalities living in the villages surrounding Gadshill, so that he preferred to disguise one place with the features of another. The graves in Pip's churchyard certainly belong to Cooling, but, according to W. Laurence Gadd's most thorough and scholarly

---

* Mrs Joe appears, in the light of modern psychiatric knowledge, to be a typical case of sexual frustration, resentful of gentle Joe because he cannot provide her with the male domination she needs, and of Pip because he has been foisted on her in place of the children she has never had. Hence her incessant 'rampaging'. Hesketh Pearson, in his book *Dickens: his Character, Comedy and Career*, remarks that although Dickens had no medical training and wrote at a time when practically nothing was known of neurosis, the neuro-psychiatrist W. Russell Brain said that his descriptions of nervous symptoms 'are so detailed and accurate that they can justly be compared with those given by clinicians of genius'. The case of Mrs Joe is an admirable illustration of this, as Pearson observes.

examination of the geography of the book,* the village was Lower Higham, and the forge at Chalk on the corner of the Dover Road and the little lane leading towards Singlewell and Cobham. The picturesque old cottage, with its long sloping tiled roof and weather-boarded front twined with roses, is still to be seen, looking a little uncertain of itself but standing up bravely to time and the awful examples of 'improvement' which surround it. It has lost its garden; a few structural alterations have taken place inside, though not many. The old anvil is still in the forge, the ring to which horses were tied for shoeing hangs by the door. The owner told the present authors that he wished he had as many shillings as the times he had seen horses shod there in the old days; it is his deep regret that cars, not horses, now occupy the stables at the back. He is proud of the commemorative plaque on the house-front, and has decked an adjoining window with small bas-reliefs of Dickensian characters.

The old Red Royal Dover Road between Gravesend and Ro-chester howls with traffic, in particular with transports on their way to and from the cement works in the Isle of Grain, and their dust spoils once-rural air. Dickens, always irritated by dust, would have had to find an adjective even more descriptive than his favourite 'gritty' for it. Bungaloid growths and houses of all grades of ugliness built between the wars have made Chalk something far different from the honeymoon hamlet, though the church whose drunken carving Dickens always saluted still has a pleasantly countrified look, and the merry drinker is none the worse for the passage of the last hundred years. It is still possible to walk in the lanes radiating from the main road, towards Cooling and Cliffe and Shorne and the Hoo villages, and there are still stretches of comparatively open country to be found, but one must be prepared for the incessant whizzing of cars and lorries past one in the narrow lanes, an irritation which would have made Dickens's walking marathons impossible. The marches are no longer mysterious, the villages no longer lonely. The great oil refinery on the Isle of Grain, the cement factories, the railway and the car have made the area one in which Dickens would not nowadays dream of settling.

Other identifications of the *Great Expectations* landmarks made

* W. Laurence Gadd, *The Great Expectations Country.*

by the ingenious Mr Gadd are the Chequers Inn (now rebuilt) at Lower Higham as the original of the Three Jolly Bargemen where Joe liked to smoke a pipe of an evening, and where a mysterious person who stirred his drink with a file presented Pip with two greasy pound notes. Lower Higham Church has a timber steeple corresponding to what Pip saw when the convict turned him upside-down, and in other ways, including its (then) remoteness from the village, which Pip describes as 'a mile or more from the church', seems suitable for the setting of Chapter One. But the little tombs belong to Cooling, and Cooling church also has a small steeple. The old Battery at Cliffe has gone, demolished about 1870; it was on the site of Cliffe fort. The pirate's gibbet is no more, nor is the prison ship, which Dickens remembered from his childhood days in Chatham, when he saw the manacled convicts. Nelson's *Euryalus* was one of these hulks, fallen on evil days after former glories; but the one Dickens describes as lying at Egypt Bay was actually the coastguard hulk. Standing in the high churchyard of Chalk, on a fine clear day, one may turn from contemplation of the cheerful grotesque over the door to the distant prospect of the river beyond the graves and the marches, and see something very like what Dickens saw: a vessel whose hull might be that of one of the old ships, riding at anchor on the silver-grey ribbon of the Thames. This churchyard, like Cooling, has all too many memorials to child victims of the marshes. Dickens's friendly carving looks down on the table-tomb of 'the four sons of Thomas and Mary Baker, (viz.) Edward, Edward, Bing and Tamsin, who died in Infancy'. The Hoo Peninsula may have lost something in remoteness, but it has certainly gained in healthiness.

When, with Pip's first visit to Miss Havisham, the story moves to Rochester, Dickens is utterly at home. He was living only four miles away and must often have gone into the town to renew his old friendship with it and build up the background to *Great Expectations*. Today he would find virtually unchanged the Crispin and Crispianus Inn at the foot of Strood Hill, with its sign of the Two Boiled Brothers, changed to less enigmatic representations of the shoemaker saints.

The bar-room of the Crispin is refreshingly unspoilt, very much as he would have seen it: the big, ancient fireplace, in which the flames must have beckoned to many a traveller on a winter's night, has a roasting-jack suspended over it. The high-backed settle with

132

the narrow seat, in a corner of which he would sit and refresh himself after one of his tremendous walks, saying little but taking in with his bright darting eyes all that was going on about him, used to be by the window, according to an old photograph. The landlady of the inn in about 1903 used to explain that this was 'because from there he would see the passers by the window; and how more than once when a poor weary woman with a couple of children has limped past, he has called them in, paid for their refreshment, and sent them away rejoicing with a shilling or two'. Because of slight structural alterations to the room the settle has been moved to a corner by the fireplace; above it are a framed bas-relief bust of Dickens and decorative plates wreathed with his characters. Here, as everywhere, there is immense pride in his association with the place. It is mentioned in his essay 'Tramps' in *The Uncommercial Traveller*.

The bridge over which one enters Rochester now is not the beautiful stone one on which Mr Pickwick meditated before breakfast; that was blown up and demolished in 1857, and the present steel bridge was built in 1911. It is about as ugly as a bridge can be. A balustrade from the one Dickens loved was presented to him by the contractors ('very nicely', as he said) and turned into a sundial for his Gadshill garden. That other nearby bridge, carrying the M2 motorway, would astonish him utterly.

The impressive ruins of Rochester Castle are much as he saw them, but the Cathedral of his time had a square grey tower; the conical hat it wears today is a copy of Bishop Gundulph's lead-covered pointed roof. Entering the High Street from the bridge end (which he could do only on foot, for it is one-way to traffic) he would find Pip's Blue Boar still there; it is, of course, the Bull of Dickens's day, the much-modernized Royal Victoria and Bull of ours. In the coffee-room (now a bar) on the left, Pip was surprised to read in a newspaper handed to him by a waiter that Pumblechook was the founder of his fortunes, and here he talked with the odious Bentley Drummle. The commercial room, on the opposite side, is now the Steak Bar, and the Great Expectations Bar, with its astonishing array of Victoriana, is appropriately below what would be Pip's bedroom when, after his fortunes were fallen, he found the Boar less welcoming than it had been, and was relegated to a bedroom 'among the pigeons and postchaises up the yard', overlooking what is now the car park.

The Guildhall where Pip was apprenticed to Joe Gargery (it is topped by a gilded weather-vane in the form of H.M.S. *Rodney*) stands as sturdy and beautiful as ever; how beautiful Dickens gives his readers no idea, for it was built in 1687 and comes into the category of 'quaint' or 'queer' by his judgment. On the opposite side is a chemist's shop, not far from the Bull, which was once the coach office of Edwards and Chaplin, where Pip would have booked his seat for London after buying his new clothes from Mr Trabb. The coach was the Nelson, and ran to the Spreadeagle, Gracechurch Street, though Pip says that he arrived at the Cross Keys in Wood Street, Cheapside—this was, of course, because the young Dickens had arrived there by Timpson's Blue-Eyed Maid.

Farther down, on the same side, built in 1684 and once a single house, is a row of three impressive gabled houses, now shops. Here was Mr Pumblechook's shop 'of a peppercorny and farinaceous character, as the premises of a corn-chandler and seedsman should be', and in fact when Dickens was writing *Great Expectations* there was a seedsman called Fairbairn in possession, whom residents remembered as having rows of little seed-drawers behind his counter. Pip thought Mr Pumblechook 'must be a very happy man indeed, to have so many little drawers in his shop'. One of the little windows set in the gables was that of Pip's little bedroom, the 'attic with a sloping roof'.

If one takes literally Pip's description of Miss Havisham's residence as being 'of old brick, and dismal' it is a pleasant surprise to turn the corner into Maidstone Road and find, opposite the Vines (the old Monk's Vineyard, now a park), a solemnly beautiful house the colour of a fading red rose. Restoration House (Dickens called it 'Satis House' after the home of Richard Watts in Boley Hill, nearby) was built in 1567, in the shape of its queen's initial, a capital E. It sheltered Charles II the night before his Restoration in May 1660. Dickens seems to have known the interior, for he describes its geography with reasonable accuracy. The 'pretty large room, well lighted with wax candles' in which Pip first met Miss Havisham is the King's Room, and in the drawing-room at the back was spread the dreadful wedding-feast with its canopy of cobwebs and mould, with spiders and mice as its wedding-guests. Restoration House fascinated Dickens. He expresses something of its allure through the mouth of Pip: 'I had stopped to look at the house as I passed, and its seared, red-bricked walls, blocked windows, and strong green ivy clasping even the stacks of chimneys with its twigs and tendons, as if with sinewy old arms, had made up a rich attractive mystery, of which I was the hero.' On 6th June 1870, only three days before his death, Dickens was seen leaning on the fence which edges the Vines, gazing intently at the house-front. Who knows what 'rich attractive mystery' would have come out of it into the pages of *Edwin Drood* if he had lived?

The courtyard before it, the side entrance by which Estella took Pip in, the 'great front entrance', are all there. But the brewery which stood by the side of the house has long been demolished ('the place will stand idle as it is, till it falls,' said Estella) and replaced by a chapel. Restoration House is a private residence, although it is open to the public once a month, and the façade may always be contemplated from the Vines, through which Pip passed on his last visit to Miss Havisham.

'The best light of the day was gone when I passed along the quiet, echoing courts behind the High Street. The nooks of ruin where the old monks had once had their refectories and gardens, and where the strong walls were now pressed into the service of humble sheds and stables, were almost as silent as the old monks in their graves. The Cathedral chimes had at once a sadder and a more remote sound to me, as I hurried on avoiding observation, than they had ever had before; so, the swell of the old organ was borne to my ears like funeral music; and the rooks, as they hovered about the grey tower and swung in the bare, high trees of the Priory garden, seemed to call to me that the place was changed, and that Estella was gone out of it for ever.'

Rochester, to Pip, was a very different place from the Rochester of Mr Pickwick. The facetiousness has gone out of Dickens's descriptions. Antiquity is significant to him of the moving-on of time, of the change in human fortunes, which in turn changes the aspect of buildings and scenes. 'Ruin . . . silent . . . sad . . . remote' are the key-words of the description.

They do not apply to Rochester a century after his death. The echoing courts have gone, the Cathedral chimes and the rooks' cawing are inaudible by day because of the inexpressible din of traffic in the High Street and behind it. The narrow street is a funnel of sound and fumes; the ancient houses seem to shudder with disgust. Driving or walking are equally unnerving experiences; pausing outside the entrance of the Bull, one feels in imminent danger of being precipitated at the lightest touch in front of the steady stream of heavy traffic pouring up from Chatham towards the bridge, while crossing at rush-hour from Pumblechook's shop to the Eastgate Museum is a hazard to be undertaken only by the swift and sure-footed. No doubt the one-way system in the High Street is all that can be done at present, but one hopes fervently that in future some way will be found to isolate all that is beautiful and historic in Rochester—the High Street, the Cathedral and Castle, and the region behind them—from the destruction of their fabric and of the peace which used to be theirs. The ugliness which surrounds the old town is, one fears, past repeal.

London plays second fiddle to Rochester in *Great Expectations*, as it now did in Dickens's life. Much of Pip's London has changed beyond recognition. Little Britain retains no flavour of Mr Jaggers; Smithfield is (mercifully) no longer 'the shameful place . . . all asmear with filth and fat and blood and foam' which had seemed to stick to the newly arrived boy; the grim bulk of Newgate no longer blocks the view of St Paul's dome. St Bartholomew's, near which lived the 'hown brother to Habraham Latheruth, on thuthpition of plate', who was one of Jaggers's most satisfied clients, has kept its fabric and its old glory, protected, perhaps, by Rahere, the jester-saint who was its founder.

One of the most delightful residences in the whole world of Dickens is Wemmick's Castle, a 'little wooden cottage in the midst of plots of garden, and the top of it was cut out and painted like a battery mounted with guns', says Pip. 'I think it was the smallest house I ever saw; with the queerest gothic windows (by far the greater part of them sham) and a gothic door, almost too small to get in at.' It had a real flagstaff, with a real flag, run up on Sundays, a bridge drawn up medieval fashion when the house's master had crossed it, a gun which fired at nine every night, Greenwich time, and (most desirable of features) a bower. 'Our punch was cooling in an ornamental lake, on whose margin the bower was raised. This piece of water (with an island in the middle which might have been the salad for supper) was of a circular form, and he had constructed a fountain in it, which, when you set a little mill going and took a cork out of a pipe, played to that

powerful extent that it made the back of your hand quite wet.'
This charming place was not in Highgate, or Hampstead, or
Greenwich, but in Walworth, perhaps near the junction of the way
to Greenwich and the Old Kent Road. Then (Dickens is writing of
a pre-Pickwick time, about 1820) Walworth was a somewhat
featureless area of market-gardens and scattered small dwellings.
To find the Castle now would be a hopeless quest; in all probability it never existed outside Dickens's fancy. But the church
where Wemmick and Miss Skiffins were married ('Halloa! here's
a church. Let's go in.') is thought to have been the old church of
St Giles, Camberwell.

More important in *Great Expectations* than the buildings is the
river. To collect material for Pip's attempt to smuggle Magwitch
out of the country, Dickens chartered a steamer from Blackwall
to Southend in May 1861, and took a party of friends and relations
with him for a picnic—'but his sleepless observation was at work
all the time' amid the laughter and the cold fowl and bottled ale.

The landmarks of that hazardous journey remain; but old
London Bridge went in 1824, and the 'race and fall of water . . .
which gave it a bad reputation', known to Elizabethan watermen,
went with it. There was little steam-traffic on the Thames then,
says Pip, and the watermen's boats were far more numerous. The
house, 'with a wooden front and three stories of bow windows' on
Mill Pond Bank, where Magwitch waited to be collected, was at
Rotherhithe, west of the Surrey Commercial Docks, and may have
been a memory of the house of Dickens's godfather Christopher
Huffam at Limehouse. One may follow Pip on that voyage, from
the Temple Stairs to Canvey Island, and the tragic end of the
rescue attempt; W. Laurence Gadd describes it in immense
detail, signposting the way for would-be explorers. But the river
conditions are as different now, and would be as unrecognizable to
Dickens, as would the inland coast at (say) Gray's Thurrock, where
the Dartford Tunnel emerges into what was in Pip's day farm-
land and heath where legends of Turpin were still told, and is now
remarkably like a geographical foretaste of hell.

11

The Public Performer

In the winter of 1861–2 he went on one of his provincial reading tours. It brought him in money, helped to satisfy his craving for activity and change, and brought about the fulfilment of his need to act. Simple properties, a limited but perfectly rehearsed programme, and his own amazing dramatic powers attracted overwhelming success everywhere he travelled. Berwick, on the Scottish Border, Norwich and Lancaster, Bury St Edmunds, Cheltenham, Carlisle and Hastings, Plymouth and Birmingham, Canterbury and Torquay, Preston and Ipswich, Manchester and Brighton, Colchester and Dover, Newcastle and Chester, all flocked to his impersonations of the Pickwickians, Tiny Tim, the Peerybingles, Scrooge. It was, said the admiring Thomas Carlyle, 'a whole trajic [sic], comic, heroic *theatre* visible, performing under one hat'.

Much of his tour was on familiar ground. The western towns of Plymouth and Torquay were probably new to him. But he had been even farther west many years before, in 1842, on a holiday trip in Cornwall, exploring the regions 'consecrated by the legends of Arthur': visiting Tintagel, climbing Mount St Michael (which is mentioned in *A Child's History of England*), gasping at Forster's temerity in mounting the Logan Stone with its terrifying sway. He had intended to open *Martin Chuzzlewit* in Cornwall, but the idea had been shelved and the county appears only in 'A Message from the Sea', one of the *Christmas Stories*.

138

Lancaster had been the scene of an excursion in 1857, after he had written to Wilkie Collins: 'I want to cast about whether you and I can go anywhere—take any tour—see anything—whereon we could write something together? Have you any idea tending to any place in the world? Will you rattle your head and see if there is any pebble in it which we could wander away and play at marbles with?' The result was the journey described in *The Uncommercial Traveller* as 'The Lazy Tour of Two Idle Apprentices'. It began with a trip to the Lake District, Dickens having read of 'some promising moors and bleak places thereabout'. They found Carlisle 'congenially and delightfully idle', the main diversion in prospect there being a lecture on India, the streets notable in the cool of the evening for promenading teenagers. Dickens noted with interest the local courting habits. 'Sometimes . . . a young man advanced behind a young woman for whom he appeared to have a tenderness, and hinted to her that he was there and playful, by giving her (he wore clogs) a kick.'

Fourteen miles away, at Hesket Newmarket, they climbed Carrock Fell 'in the exaggerative mist', arriving at the top to get 'a magnificent view of—Nothing!' From Wigton they went on to Allonby, where they stayed at the Ship, 'a capital little homely inn', but Allonby reminded Dickens 'of what Broadstairs might have been if it had not inherited a cliff, and had been an Irishman'. Then, en route for Doncaster and its races, they paused in Lancaster, where Thomas Idle (the pseudonym of Collins) had heard there was a good old inn, 'established in a fine old house; an inn where they give you Bride-cake every day after dinner. Let us eat Bride-cake without the trouble of being married, or of knowing anybody in that ridiculous dilemma'. Collins had, in fact, no intention of going to that trouble, being perfectly content with a mistress, and Dickens was feeling the dilemma to be particularly ridiculous at that moment of his history.

Lancaster had an abundance of good old inns. In 1857 and 1862, when Dickens knew it, it was indeed 'a pleasant place . . . dropped in the midst of a charming landscape, a place with a fine ancient fragment of castle, a place of lovely walks, a place possessing staid old houses richly fitted with old Honduras mahogany, which has grown so dark with time that it seems to have got something of a retrospective mirror-quality into itself, and to show the visitor, in the depth of its grain, through all its polish, the hue of the wretched slaves who groaned long ago under old Lancaster merchants'.

Communications and industry have turned the litle grey town, once so snug, into something bigger and uglier than Dickens saw. The scent of linoleum is heavy on the air, late Victorian and twentieth-century buildings have over-weighted its narrow streets, but on the whole it has changed less, and kept more of its atmospheric antiquity, than most towns. The castle (considerably more than 'a fragment') still dominates the skyline with its old threat and mystery; Horseshoe Corner has embedded in its modern road-surface a horseshoe commemorating one cast by the steed of the castle's master, John of Gaunt, in the fourteenth century. Round the beautiful Priory Church on the Castle Hill still cluster the houses of the Lancaster merchants who made their money out of the slave-trade, and less grand but equally ancient houses abound all over the town and by the River Lune. Dickens could still find today lovely walks along the river and in the wild beautiful Trough of Bowland. But he would not find the King's Arms he knew, 'a very remarkable old house . . . with genuine old rooms and an uncommonly quaint staircase' where he had 'a state bedroom with two enormous red fourposters in it, each as big as Charley's room at Gadshill'. The inn is described in more detail in 'The Lazy Tour' as having 'a certain grave mystery lurking in the depth of the old mahogany panels, as if they were so many deep pools of dark water'. Panels and staircase and all went in 1879, when the old King's Arms was pulled down and replaced by the present hotel, the Royal King's Arms. At the same time the management ceased to serve the bride-cake about which the curious ghost story in 'The Lazy Tour' revolves. Whether, in fact, a young bride had been poisoned at the inn and her lover slain with a billhook by her slave-trader husband, who later was hanged for the double crime at Lancaster Castle, there is no knowing. It is a legend which would attract Dickens; but it may well have originated in his fancy.

He really had no need to invent instances of the supernatural, having in his own being so much of it. At Doncaster races he (who was quite uninvolved with horses, form, or gambling of any kind) acquired a race card and wrote down, for fun, the names of three winners. 'And if you can believe it, without your hair standing on end,' he told Forster, 'those three races were won, one after another, by those three horses!'

Provincial backgrounds found no place in *Our Mutual Friend*, the novel he was writing in 1864. He was established at Gadshill, with no thought of leaving it for more than brief periods, such as his foray to France because 'I had certainly worked myself into a damaged state'. Damaged, indeed, he was by overwork, domestic worries about the future of his children, and by more personal emotional troubles. A recurrent, painful lameness in his left foot was the first sign of the thrombosis which lay in wait for him. He needed more and more money, rich though he was, for the support of his many dependants, and he must go on writing; not that he was ever in any danger of retiring, so fertile was his brain and so feverish his energies.

Our Mutual Friend was to be about 'a man, young and perhaps eccentric, feigning to be dead, and *being* dead to all intents and purposes external to himself, and for years retaining the singular view of life and character so imparted'. This was John Rokesmith, supposed drowned. London River flows through the book more strongly than through any other. Odorous, sinister, relentless, it gives Rogue Riderhood his unpleasant living (his very cap looks 'like a furry animal, dog or cat, puppy or kitten, drowned and decaying') around the bridges of London, in the watery world which had always lured Dickens, and which he now knew so well through his association with the river police. It provides Gaffer Hexam with whatever he may dredge up from it in the pockets of the drowned: 'Has a dead man to have money . . . ? How can money be a corpse's?' Mortimer Lightwood and Eugene Wrayburn go to inspect one of these gruesome finds 'down by the Monument, and by the Tower, and by the Docks; down by Ratcliff and by Rotherhithe; down by where accumulated scum of humanity seemed to be washed from higher grounds, like so much moral sewage'. The Hexam dwelling had been a windmill, in the long-past days when the Thames had such things along its banks. This is not the river of the earlier *Dombey and Son* with its merchandise and spices, or of the visits to Christopher Huffam. It is sordid and threatening, even in its evidence of a more picturesque past: 'Not a figure-head but had the menacing look of bursting forward to run them down.'

Few relics of the river of 1864 remain as they were. The growth of the docks, which was beginning in Dickens's youth, the spread of population and industry, have changed its face, though the squalor and the romance are still there for those who care to look

for them, just as on the grey slimy beaches there may be found
Elizabethan coins and daggers and Roman brooches, if the searcher
is extremely lucky. One building, an important one in *Our Mutual
Friend*, has survived. The Six Jolly Fellowship Porters, presided
over by the formidable Abbey Potterson, is the Grapes, Narrow
Street, Limehouse. The site of Limehouse Hole is now occupied
by Aberdeen Wharf, but Narrow Street, thanks to a timely protest
in the press, has survived to give an indication of what Dickens's
Limehouse was like. To Dickens the Grapes was 'a tavern of a
dropsical appearance . . . long settled down into a state of hale
infirmity. In its whole constitution it had not a straight floor, and
hardly a straight line; but it had outlasted, and clearly would yet
outlast, many a better-trimmed building, many a sprucer public-
house'. And so it has—and bombs besides. Its river frontage is
substantially the same as then, the building still as tall and narrow
as when Dickens compared it to 'a handle of a flat iron set upright
on its broadest end'. The bar was very small, but no one could
have wished it bigger, he said: 'That space was so girt in by cor-
pulent little casks, and by cordial bottles radiant with fictitious
grapes in bunches, and by lemons in nets, and by biscuits in
baskets, and by polite beer-pulls that made low bows when customers were served with beer.' The bar is now more commodious
and comfortable, with a television set which a modern writer *
thinks Miss Potterson would have thrown into the river. The room
at the back, overlooking the water, is the Dickens Room. What,
one wonders, would he have made of the power station which is
the Grapes's neighbour? He would certainly have enjoyed the
experience of sitting outside, eating shellfish and watching the
river-traffic, on a summer evening; and might have given way to
the temptation to mingle with the dockers who have the rare privilege of drinking at the Grapes between six and eight in the morning, by virtue of a special licence.

The upper reaches of the Thames have a place in *Our Mutual
Friend*. Mortimer Lightwood and Eugene Wrayburn have a
bachelor cottage at Hampton. Betty Higden would be unlikely to
carry on her baby-minding nowadays at a cottage as rustic as the
one shown in Marcus Stone's illustration,† or to be able to flee

* Geoffrey Fletcher: *London's River*.

† Authentic edition of Dickens's works (Chapman & Hall, 1901).

from the shadow of the workhouse through Chertsey, Walton, Kingston and Staines, 'keeping to by-ways'. The Paper Mill, where her long journey found an ending, and where Lizzie Hexam worked, is thought to be Marsh Mill, a mile or so above Henley-on-Thames, and the attempted murder of Wrayburn by Headstone would in that case have occurred on the tow· a h below Henley.

Our Mutual Friend is primarily a book about money: its power and its corrupting influence. Boffin's Bower, or Harmony Jail, where Mr Boffin acquired the golden dust which apparently changed his nature, was at Battle Bridge, on a spot covered by King's Cross Station (Boffin's 'Over Maiden Lane Way—out Holloway direction' is misleading). The golden dust-heaps ('certain dark mounds rose high against the sky') were, in fact, muck-heaps, the dumped refuse of London, composed of every kind of filth. Corporation dumps and incinerators did not exist: the idea of burying rubbish had not occurred to anyone, or if it had they would have rejected the thought as shockingly wasteful. For muck meant money. Scavengers had rich pickings from them: one heap was sold for £40,000. Dickens had already satirized the wealthy dust-contractors in an article in *Household Words*, and now he used the noisome masses as a symbol of property, and an opportunity for savage, brilliant satire. A contemporary print shows them, against a line of rickety fencing, a background of squalid tenements with smoky chimneys, and behind the tower of New St Pancras Church. The railway premises, goods depots and other paraphernalia of transport which now cover the Bower and its lucrative mounds may not be pretty, but would be a good deal more gratifying to Dickens than what he saw there in 1864. It had been even worse: a positive mountain at Battle Bridge, known as 'Mr Starkey's', had been removed in 1848.

The Wilfers, who were poor but much concerned with wealth, lived at a house in Holloway, 'north of London, and then divided from it by fields and trees. Between Battle Bridge and that part of the Holloway district in which he [Rumty Wilfer] dwelt, was a tract of suburban Sahara, where tiles and bricks were burnt, bones were boiled, carpets were beat, rubbish was shot, dogs were fought, and dust was heaped by contractors ... the light of its kiln-fires made lurid smears upon the fog.' The pleasant fields below Highgate, in which David Copperfield and Oliver Twist could have seen cows grazing at the north end of Holloway Road, has changed drastically since the 1830s. Nothing is left of rural Holloway but, here and there, a lonely, down-at-heel house which stood there before Muck and Money deprived it of its dignity. Mr Venus's shop, of eldritch fascination, is said by Dickens to be in Clerkenwell, but the 'narrow and dirty street' devoted to small eating-houses, barbers, pet-shop keepers and the like has been placed by Dickensian deduction as St Andrew Street, Seven Dials, now vanished, but not unlike the present Monmouth Street in appearance. Here, behind the dark shop-window in which nothing is clearly visible but a candle and 'two preserved frogs fighting a small-sword duel',* is Mr Venus's stock-in-trade, a shopful of bones ('Mr Wegg observes that he has a convenient little shelf near his knees, exclusively appropriated to skeleton hands, which have very much the appearance of wanting to lay hold of him'), of human and animal remains of all kinds, from a 'Hindoo baby in a bottle, curved up with his big head tucked under him' to 'a pretty little dead bird lying on the counter, with its head drooping on one side against the rim of Mr Venus's saucer, and a long stiff wire piercing its breast'. Truly, Dickens has travelled far in time and maturity, if not in geography, from Lant Street, Mr Bob Sawyer, and those jolly student jokes about borrowed arms and legs, and boys swallowing beads.

A happier metamorphosis has occurred in Smith Square, Westminster, where in a little quiet terraced house lived crippled Jenny Wren, the dolls' dressmaker, with her sottish father: it has now gone up in the world, a genteel suburb of Parliament. The 'very hideous church, with four towers at the four corners, generally resembling some petrified monster, frightful and gigantic, on its back with its legs in the air' was Archer's early eighteenth-century St John the Evangelist, Smith Square, a pleasant enough edifice before severe war damage overtook it. Dickens does not seem to have seen any place or building quite straight in *Our Mutual Friend*; there is that familiar touch of liverishness in his descriptions, as though he were indeed bilious, and everything he looked on seemed black-spotted or tinged with a sickly foggy yellow. Only one place is radiant: the Ship Tavern at Greenwich, scene of the

---

* The original of this was a French bronze group, one of those objects which Dickens liked to have near him when he was writing.

innocent elopement of Bella and her father, and of Bella's wedding-feast after her marriage with John. 'What a dinner! Specimens of all the fishes that swim in the sea, surely had swum their way to it . . . and the dishes being seasoned with Bliss—an article which they are sometimes out of, at Greenwich—were of perfect flavour, and the golden drinks had been bottled in the golden age and hoarding up their sparkles ever since.'

Dickens had been so conspicuously out of Bliss himself, throughout the book, that one wonders what caused this sudden idyllic note in his prose. Perhaps it was a memory of personal happiness, irresistible when the chance came to perpetuate it. The Ship was a favourite resort of Dickens and his friends, who would go up by water to enjoy its famous whitebait suppers of an evening.* But one may be allowed to wonder whether some happier, tenderer occasion may not have been in his mind; for Bella, surely, is a portrait of Ellen Ternan, 'Nelly', 'My Darling'. She is the first real girl he had ever portrayed. Estella of *Great Expectations* is a beautiful, cold-hearted, female torturer; perhaps this is how Ellen appeared to Dickens at the time. Bella Wilfer (Wilful?) is pretty, selfish, greedy, natural, amusing, naughty, vulnerable and human. Those poor wax dolls, the Agneses and Rose Maylies and Little Nells, have melted; now, at the age of fifty-two, he has discovered how to create a real woman, a Lovely Woman, as Bella liked to call herself. Was it Nelly who sat with a man twice her age ('Pa'?) in the little room overlooking the river, and was 'more delightful than anything else in the festival, and imagined all sorts of voyages for herself and Pa'? Home-brew psychology, perhaps, such a deduction. But, for Dickens's sake, one hopes that it was so; that the tormented, ageing genius could find even for a moment the happiness he had longed for and lacked.

In 1866 and 1867, according to the researches of Sir Felix Aylmer,† he was dividing his time between Gadshill, his bachelor apartment above the *All the Year Round* offices, and two houses in which he successively established Ellen: Elizabeth Cottage, High

---

* The Ship was destroyed in the Second World War, but its sister inn the Trafalgar Tavern has been restored to even more than its former splendour; whitebait and 'all the fishes that swim in the sea' are still notably served there in august maritime surroundings.

† *Dickens Incognito.*

Street, Slough, on a site now occupied by shops, and Windsor Lodge, Linden Grove, Nunhead, Peckham.* Before these moves, Sir Felix conjectures, Ellen may have lived at a house called Elm View or Elm Villa, in Selwood Place, Fulham Road, where Dickens himself had lodged when courting Kate Hogarth.

On 2nd September 1865 he wrote a 'Postscript in lieu of Preface' to *Our Mutual Friend*. 'On Friday the ninth of June in the present year Mr and Mrs Boffin (in their manuscript dress of receiving Mr and Mrs Lammle at breakfast) were on the South-Eastern Railway with me, in a terribly destructive accident. When I had done what I could to help others, I climbed back into my carriage—nearly turned over a viaduct, and caught aslant upon the turn—to extricate the worthy couple. They were much soiled, but otherwise unhurt. The same happy result attended Miss Bella Wilfer on her wedding-day, and Mr Riderhood inspecting Bradley Headstone's red neckerchief as he lay asleep. I remember with devout thankfulness that I can never be much nearer parting company with my readers for ever, than I was then, until there shall be written against my life the two words with which I have this day closed the book—THE END.'

There is no sign at the mid-Kent village of Staplehurst of the railway accident which spared Dickens's life but ruined his nerves, and made train travel, which he had formerly enjoyed, a purgatory to him. It had occurred on his favourite line, the South-Eastern to Folkestone,† when he was returning from a holiday in France. Ellen may have been with him, but there is no concrete evidence of this. It has been deduced that the dramatic death of Mr Carker under the wheels of a train happened at Paddock Wood: ironic that the 'iron monster' which was an instrument in Dickens's own destruction should have met with disaster at a point so near. In 1867 he was writing to Georgina, from Liverpool, where he had been giving a reading: 'I am not quite right within, but believe it to be an effect of the railway shaking. There is no doubt of the fact that, after the Staplehurst experience, it tells more and more (railway shaking, that is) instead of, as one might have expected, less and less.' Railways had advanced since the early, slow,

* Also demolished.

† 'Where he was known to every guard, porter and station-master, who could be seen flying to open the door for him,' says Forster.

hazardous days. Speed spelt success and progress to these mid Victorians. 'Now, every fool in Buxton can be in Bakewell in half an hour and every fool in Bakewell in Buxton', complained Ruskin, to whom such things meant nothing, for he was a contemplative with neither need nor desire to rush up and down the country. The fine, efficient express trains were indispensable to Dickens on his reading tours, which were very closely programmed. But after his sufferings early in the 1867 tour, travelling to Glasgow by way of Liverpool and Manchester, his manager Dolby reports that 'it was decided between us that, so far as practicable, we would in future travel by slow trains. The plan seemed to dispel his nervousness to a great extent; but it had to be given up, as the delay and the monotony of these journeys were almost worse than the shaking of the expresses.' By only a few years Dickens missed the coming of the Pullmans, which would have made travel so much pleasanter for him. However much he might suffer, his spirit was unbroken. On the way back to London from the last Scottish reading, at Edinburgh, when there was no time for dinner before leaving, big simple Dolby was entertained en route by Mr Dickens 'with a song and dance (the drinking song from *Der Freischütz*) with glass in hand'.

He was chronically ill. He wanted to remain at Gadshill, now 'improved' to his liking, and pass his time entertaining his friends and enjoying Kentish pleasures. But relentless persuasion from Fields in America, and the lure of £10,000, drew him across the Atlantic on a mammoth tour. He was away from England from 9th November 1867 to May 1868. 'Good lord! seven years younger!' cried his doctor, seeing the bronzed face. But the improvement was superficial. Some of his great vitality was gone, the lightness of his step had given way to a tired, dragging gait, and the wonderful brightness of his eyes was sometimes dimmed. He did not allow any of this to show on the day when he came home, like a conquering hero, along country roads lined with waving, cheering farmers and their families, past cottages decked in his honour, to a Gadshill whose bricks were invisible behind a blaze of triumphal bunting. Prevented by Mamie from greeting her father's arrival with a resounding attack on the alarm-bell, the bell-ringers of Higham made up for it on Sunday, when they rushed out at the end of the morning sermon to 'ring like mad' for joy that Dickens was home again.

12

'The Resurrection and the Life'

'During that summer [1868] there was not a week in which he did not entertain', remembered Dolby. Longfellow and one of his daughters came over and were taken for drives in post carriages, with postilions in 'the old red jacket of the old red royal Dover road' that ran in front of Gadshill. Fechter, the actor, was there too: he it was who had sent Dickens the Swiss chalet in which he now did his writing when weather permitted. It had been a somewhat alarming present to receive, arriving from Paris in ninety-four pieces and having to be erected on an expensive brickwork foundation. But Dickens was delighted with it. 'It will really be a very pretty thing,' he wrote in January 1865, 'and in the summer (supposing it not to be blown away in the spring) the upper room will make a charming study. It is much higher than we supposed.'

It was not blown away in the spring, and in summer Dickens embellished it with five mirrors to make it lighter and more interesting, 'and they reflect and refract, in all kinds of ways, the leaves that are quivering at the windows, and the great fields of waving corn, and the sail-dotted river. My room is up among the branches of the trees; and the birds and the butterflies fly in and out, and the green branches shoot in at the open windows, and the lights and shadows of the clouds come and go with the rest of the company. The scent of the flowers, and indeed of everything that is growing for miles and miles, is most delicious.'

The chalet was set up, not in the garden proper, but in the

shrubbery (still called the Wilderness) secluded from the road, and in close company with the two magnificent cedars which had been there when Dickens was a boy. He and the family could come and go by way of the underground tunnel, without bothering to cross the road. The furnishings of the upper room of the chalet were simple: little more than his writing-desk and chair. He took a childlike pleasure in a number of little objects which he could look at when he raised his eyes from his work. In his meticulous fashion, he placed each one in the same position every day. There was the bronze group of the two frogs fighting a duel with swords, which he had introduced into *Our Mutual Friend*, another French bronze figurine representing a Parisian dog-fancier 'with a profusion of little dogs stuck under his arms and into his pockets, and everywhere where little dogs could possibly be insinuated'. There was a long gilt leaf, with a rabbit sitting up on it, a large paper-knife, which its owner liked to hold and flourish during his public readings, and a little green cup painted with cowslips, in which Georgina or Mamie would place fresh flowers every morning. Beside it stood a desk calendar.

The readings were almost at an end. In October 1868, he rashly took on a new series, which included for the first time the harrowing 'Sikes and Nancy', causing women in the audience to faint and rending the reader's nerves. Somehow he carried on, against all advice, until April; then those at home had 'ill report of him from Chester'. From the Sea-Beach Hotel * at Blackpool ('charming!' he commented), he wrote: 'I have had a delicious walk by the sea today, and I sleep soundly, and have picked up amazingly in appetite. My foot is greatly better too, and I wear my own boot.' †
The fresh breeze blowing from the sea revived him enormously after the smoke of Leeds, Blackburn, Bolton, Preston and Warrington, where he had been reading, and he felt able after his interlude there to return to Preston, where he had another engagement to read in the Guildhall. 'Preston . . . was if possible more dirty and melancholy than usual,' said Dolby. They walked from the station to the Bull (humorously referred to by Dickens as 'the Palazzo Bull') where Dickens's doctor, F. Carr Beard, was to meet them and carry out a medical examination.

* In fact, the Imperial.

† He had suffered severely since January 1865 with swelling, inflammation and lameness in his left foot.

It lasted half an hour. Then Beard said: 'If you insist on Dickens taking the platform tonight, I will not guarantee but that he goes through life dragging a foot behind him.'

All the money paid in advance by the public had to be refunded —somehow. Dickens's agent had paid all their previous takings into the bank, and the banks were closed. The manager of the Bull came to the rescue. Mr Townsend had been station-master at Preston and knew Dickens. A kind, resourceful man, he borrowed and begged about £120, and the money was distributed in the Guildhall to those who came to ask for it. There was no trouble from anybody but 'one or two ill-conditioned persons' who complained that the illness could not be genuine, as that morning they had seen Dickens on the sands at Blackpool, 'kicking his hat about as if he had been a boy'. In fact, he had been running after it.

So ended Dickens's provincial readings, and if he had indeed satirized Preston in *Hard Times* he had now some reason to be grateful to it for Townsend's kindness and the general sympathy and forbearance of the Preston people. The Bull, now the Bull and Royal, is still one of Preston's principal hotels: it stands in Church Street.

George Dolby had become warmly attached to his 'Chief' on the series of tours for which he had been manager. Now accepted into the ranks of Dickens's personal friends, he was invited down to Gadshill to join those merry parties organized for the Americans who arrived at Gadshill 'with the nightingales' in May 1869. Mr Fields, Mr Childs, Etynge the artist, Dr Fordyce Barker of New York and Dolby had been invited by their host to take a look round 'Horrible London', under the guidance of Scotland Yard detectives. One of the interesting lairs they visited was an opium den in the Ratcliff Highway, known as Tiger Bay, where they noticed an old woman mixing the drug for her clients. 'A curious experience for our American friends' and a productive one for Dickens. In sharp contrast, 'Gad's', when they got there, was looking its very best, with trees and hedges in blossom, the fields a mass of colour with the wild flowers which have, a hundred years later, almost disappeared; and Dickens, waiting for them in a basket carriage at Higham Station, in a light suit, his hat perkily on one side shading his country-brown face, looking a different man from the one Dolby had left in London.

On the lawns at Gadshill croquet and bowls were in progress,

the bright dresses of the ladies twinkling among the scarlet uniforms of some officers from Chatham 'who had dropped in in the
course of the morning' to that hospitable house. Then there was a
jolly luncheon, and the entertainment programme began. During
the next days the guests were conducted by Dickens on a variety of
excursions. One was his favourite walk through Cobham Park,
finishing up at the Leather Bottle. Since he had taken Mr Pickwick
on the same walk, he had taken it himself many times, 'through
a deep and shady wood, cooled by the light wind . . . the ivy and
the moss crept in thick clusters over the old trees, and the soft
green turf overspread the ground like a silken mat. They emerged
upon an open park, with an ancient hall, displaying the quaint
and picturesque architecture of Elizabeth's time.' This was
Cobham Hall, the scene of one of Mary Weller's ghost stories *:

'There was the daughter of the first occupier of the picturesque
Elizabethan house, so famous in our neighbourhood. You have
heard about her? No, why, *she* went out one summer evening at
twilight, when she was a beautiful girl, just seventeen years of age,
to gather flowers in the garden; and presently came running,
terrified, into the hall to her father, saying, "Oh, dear father, I
have met myself!" He took her in his arms, and told her it was
fancy, but she said, "Oh, no! I met myself in the broad walk, and
I was pale and gathering withered flowers, and I turned my head,
and held them up!" And, that night, she died; and a picture of
her story was begun, though never finished, and they say it is
somewhere in the house to this day, with its face to the wall.'

Cobham Hall, like Gadshill, is now a school for girls; but its
grounds and house are open at certain times to visitors to follow
the footsteps of Dickens. The walk from Gadshill through
Cobham Park to the Leather Bottle was a long one, with his
ailing foot, but he enjoyed every inch of it, not least the arrival at
the snug little inn which he was so proud to show off to his
American guests. There was the very parlour in which the love-
lorn Tupman had recuperated on roast fowl and bacon; there were
the same dark old portraits and crude bright prints; there was the
real leather bottle of immense antiquity (now hanging in the bar),
which had been discovered filled with gold coins during alterations to the inn. Through the window you could see the high-

* Retold by Dickens in *Christmas Stories* from *Household Words* (1850).

151

perched old church, where Pickwick and his young friend had paced among the graves in earnest conversation. And upstairs, in the low-ceilinged little bedroom with the lattice window, Mr Pickwick, unable to sleep and in 'a nervous and excited state', had read the Madman's Manuscript given to him by the clergyman at Dingley Dell, and thereby made himself considerably more nervous and excited.

Then there was ale all round, and the Americans toasted Dickens and he toasted them, and (though Dolby does not say so, being used to the radiant smile and infectious laughter of his Chief) there on the ale-bench Dickens must have sat, beaming on the company, and looking, as he had said of Mr Tupman in that same room, 'as unlike a man who had taken his leave of the world, as possible'. Neither he nor any of that genial company can have guessed how soon he would take it.

Even when the weather was unsuitable for Cobham, Dickens would neither stay in himself nor let his guests do so; they must stride on misty walks to the marshes at Cooling to savour the true atmosphere of *Great Expectations*, or drive the twenty-nine miles to Canterbury. Again the two post-carriages were hired, and the scarlet-jacketed postilions. Hampers and wine baskets blocked the house-porch on their way out, everyone chattered and laughed and shared Dickens's excitement. 'We travelled merrily over the road, with hop gardens on either side, until we reached Rochester, our horses making such a clatter in this slumbrous old city that all the shopkeepers in the main street turned out to see us pass.' They came to Canterbury just as the Cathedral bells were ringing for Evensong. 'Entering the quiet city under the old gate * at the end of the High Street, it seemed as though its inhabitants were indulging in an afternoon's nap after a midday dinner. But our entry and the clatter of our horses' hoofs roused them as it had done the people of Rochester, and they came running to their windows and out into the streets to learn what so much noise might mean.'

While the horses rested in the stables of the Fountain Hotel the party attended Evensong, which they thought badly conducted and which Dickens criticized sharply. He decided to elevate his spirits by acting as guide, 'after he had politely but speedily got

* The West Gate.

rid of a tedious verger who wanted to lead the way'; and a very curious view of English history those Americans must have been given. They were disappointed that Dickens was not similarly enthusiastic in pointing out the scenes from *David Copperfield*: he laughingly eluded their questions.

On another day he would take them to Rochester on a sight-seeing tour of its antiquities. His guests were not let into the secret that from the scenes so familiar to him 'a very curious and new idea' was germinating in his brain. In July he wrote to Forster about it: 'the story was to be that of the murder of a nephew by his uncle; the originality of which was to consist in the review of the murderer's career by himself at the close, when its temptations were to be dwelt upon as if, not he the culprit, but some other man, were the tempted ... all discovery of the murderer was to be baffled till towards the close, when, by means of a gold ring which has resisted the corrosive effects of the lime into which he had thrown the body, not only the person murdered was to be identified but the locality of the crime and the man who committed it.'

In the autumn of 1869 the plot, its convolutions and development, mind-pictures of the characters and the settings, were whirling round in his head together with the routine work for *All the Year Round*, the preparation of twelve farewell readings to be given in London, and the composition of an Inaugural Address to be given at the Town Hall, Birmingham, on 27th September, in his capacity as President of the Midland Institute. By the end of the third week in October he had finished the first number of the book, titled with much difficulty *The Mystery of Edwin Drood*.* During the early months of 1870, while the readings were in progress, he was writing at the house he had rented from his friend Milner Gibson, No. 5 Hyde Park Place. He wrote to Fields in America: 'We live here (opposite the Marble Arch) in a charming house until the 1st of June, and then return to Gad's ... I have a large room here, with three fine windows, overlooking the Park,

---

* The choice of a name for the character and a title for the book seem to have given Dickens unusual trouble, judging by his notes for the novel. He toyed with many possibilities, including *The Loss of James Wakefield*, *James's Disappearance, Flight and Pursuit, The Loss of Edwyn Brood, The Mystery in the Drood Family, The Flight of Edwyn Drood, Dead? or Alive?* The name of Edwin Drood is said to have been derived from that of the landlord of the Falstaff Inn, opposite Gadshill Place, a Mr Trood.

unsurpassable for airiness and cheerfulness.' The house, his last London lodging, has disappeared along with so much else that surrounded Marble Arch.

By the end of May he was where he must have longed to be, back at 'Gad's'. He had been through a period of intense mental and physical strain, and 'seemed very weary', his anxious family thought. But he complained little, and went on subjecting himself to his usual strenuous exercise. On Monday 6th June, he walked with his letters for the post into Rochester. There somebody noticed him leaning on the fence at the Maidstone Road (then Crow Lane) entrance to the Vines, gazing at Restoration House as though fixing its every feature in his memory. Was it to have a place in *Edwin Drood*? Almost certainly, for it had been Satis House in *Great Expectations*, and the localities of that book and of earlier stories and papers were reappearing in the new one.* Mr Pumblechook's house and shop had become the premises of Mr Sapsea, auctioneer and Mayor of Cloisterham (Rochester). No little enviable drawers to be found in it now: it is 'irregularly modernized here and there, as steadily deteriorating generations found, more and more, that they preferred air and light to Fever and the Plague. Over the doorway is a wooden effigy, about half life-size, representing Mr Sapsea's father, in a curly wig and toga, in the act of selling. The chastity of the idea, and the natural appearance of the little finger, hammer, and pulpit, have been much admired.' This figure actually existed, and Dickens knew it well, though it was over a house in St Margaret's Banks, not in the position he describes. In his boyhood he may have been one of those youths who made repeated attacks on it, but found it too firmly fixed to be removed.

Eastgate House, almost opposite 'Sapsea's', a fine gabled building of late Tudor date, had escaped Dickens's attentions except for a possible mention in *The Pickwick Papers* as the Westgate House of the Bury St Edmunds' adventure. Now he transformed it into 'the Nuns' House, a venerable brick edifice, whose present appellation is doubtless derived from the legend of its conventual uses. On the trim gate enclosing its old courtyard is a resplendent brass plate flashing forth the legend: "Seminary for Young

* Though Watt's Charity of 'The Seven Poor Travellers' (*Christmas Stories*) does not find a place up to the point of the story Dickens had reached at his death.

Ladies. Miss Twinkleton".' Miss Twinkleton educates and boards Miss Rosa Bud, the orphan girl betrothed to Edwin Drood and passionately loved by his uncle, John Jasper, the choirmaster of the Cathedral. Like Bella Wilfer, she is a real girl: younger and sillier than Bella, but capable of human feelings, made of flesh and blood. She gets her fingers and her mouth sticky with the wares at the 'Lumps of Delight' sweet-shop in the High Street, a thing no previous Dickens heroine would ever have done, on any account.

Jasper lodges at the little gatehouse, the College Gatehouse in High Street, some way down from the Bull, 'crossing the Close, with an arched thoroughfare passing beneath it. Through its latticed window, a fire shines out upon the fast-darkening scene.' The lair of the spider Jasper is an innocuous-seeming little lair; the sinister postern stair up which the three guests at that mysterious Christmas dinner went, each to his fate, is concealed behind a door. Beneath it, in the official residence of Mr Tope the verger, Jasper's landlord, you may take coffee or lunch or tea, or buy the present-day equivalent of Lumps of Delight. Mr Datchery, the enigmatic stranger to Cloisterham, lodged there, and thought it 'partook of the character of a cool dungeon'. The 'chambers of no describable shape' are, in fact, beautiful old rooms enriched by fine linenfold panelling and what estate agents call a wealth of exposed beams, and are certainly venerable and architectural, as Datchery wished his accommodation to be; but hardly, as he also stipulated, inconvenient.

Minor Canon Row, called in the book Minor Canon Corner, is 'a wonderfully quaint row of red-brick tenements . . . they had odd little porches over the doors, like sounding-boards over old pulpits'. Thus he describes the Row in an earlier story, 'The Seven Poor Travellers'. In *Edwin Drood* it becomes 'a quiet place in the shadow of the Cathedral, which the cawing of the rooks, the echoing footsteps of rare passers, the sound of the Cathedral bell, or the roll of the Cathedral organ, seemed to render more quiet than absolute silence'. The Minor Canon who could enjoy absolute silence in the Row today would be fortunate indeed, as was the hearty, athletic Canon Crisparkle who lived there with his pretty mother, like a Dresden shepherdess in her daintiness, and the dark strange Landless twins. Dickens had known a house in the Row in his childhood which contained just such a wonderful dining-room closet as that in which Mrs Crisparkle kept so many extraordinary revivers and remedies: Constantia and home-made biscuits, pickles, spices and jams, oranges and sugar and sweet wine and home-made cordials.

From Minor Canon Row one crosses the Vines, emerging at Restoration House. A little farther up the road was 'The Travellers' Twopenny', where the urchin Deputy lodged. Once a pub called the White Duck, later Kitt's Lodging House, it is the only *Edwin Drood* landmark to have vanished. In the Vines (called the Monks' Vineyard, which it actually had been) the doomed Edwin meets the old opium woman, and is puzzled and disturbed by her searching questions. Is he engaged? Is his name Eddy? If so, he is threatened, mortally threatened. The woman, 'Princess Puffer', is based on the drug-mixing old woman whom Dickens and Fields had encountered during the 1869 tour of 'Horrible London'.

As to the Crozier, where Mr Datchery put up with a view to taking lodgings in Cloisterham, it must be the Bull, with a new name, borrowed from the Mitre in Chatham. It is 'the orthodox hotel'. But Dickens places it somewhere more obscure than its actual position: it is 'an hotel of a most retiring disposition', and Datchery gets lost and bewildered in his search for Tope's, which was actually just down the street from the Bull.

What the Thames was to *Our Mutual Friend*, the Cathedral is to *Edwin Drood*. Death and burial, or apparent death and concealment, are the theme of the latter: 'if Drood is dead there is no mystery about him', it has been said, and the ability of the sexton Durdles to detect 'old 'uns' within crypts and vaults by tapping the walls may only mean that *a* body will be discovered, corroded to nothing by quicklime, with a gold ring twinkling among the ashes to denounce the murderer. But a place of tombs was required for the crime, or apparent crime, and Rochester Cathedral had always symbolized mortality to Dickens, from Jingle onwards: 'Sarcophagus—fine place—old legends too—strange stories—capital.' In *Edwin Drood* the emphasis is stronger. 'A monotonous, silent city, deriving an earthy flavour through from its Cathedral crypt, and so abounding in vestiges of monastic graves, that the Cloisterham children grow small salad in the dust of abbots and abbesses, and make dirt-pies of nuns and friars.' In Dickens's day it was no doubt common for human remains to be discovered when a Rochester house was demolished, or rebuilt, or a garden was dug or a field ploughed, and his strongly anti-Roman sentiments found no particular cause for reverence to be paid to the bones of pre-Reformation ecclesiastics. He was fond of the Cathedral, 'a little vain of it', like its townsmen, in spite of its deplorable past, and fascinated by its atmosphere, which he conveys in *Edwin Drood* with a flowing lyricism unlike anything in his previous prose:

'"Dear me," said Mr Grewgious, peeping in, "it's like looking down the throat of Old Time."

'Old Time heaved a mouldy sigh from tomb and arch and vault; and gloomy shadows began to deepen in corners; and damps began to rise from great patches of stone; and jewels, cast upon the pavement of the nave from stained glass by the declining sun, began to perish. . . . In the free outer air, the river, the green pastures and the brown arable lands, the teeming hills and dales, were reddened by the sunset; while the distant little windows in windmills and farm homesteads, shone, patches of bright beaten gold. In the Cathedral, all became gray, murky, and sepulchral, and the cracked monotonous mutter went on like a dying voice, until the organ and the choir burst forth, and drowned it in a sea of music. Then, the sea fell, and the dying voice made another feeble effort, and then the sea rose high, and beat its life out, and lashed the roof, and surged among the arches, and pierced the heights of the great tower; and then the sea was dry, and all was still.'

Perhaps Old Time has worked for the better in the Cathedral, for today it is a light, cheerful, welcoming place, its interior architecturally undistinguished, but adorned with some pleasant Georgian monuments featuring large, lush, classical ladies. On a recent visit (1969) the mutter of a voice could indeed be heard at Evensong time, to be answered by another voice; but no sea of music drowned them, for the service was being celebrated without organ, choir, or congregation, and visitors roamed the nave while it was in progress. Perhaps Mr Grewgious really meant that the Crypt resembles the throat of Old Time—its arches could be said to recall the great open mouth of a whale. It is cool and dark compared with what one has left above; it seems more ancient and ghostly. On window-sills are propped tomb-ornaments of marble, little skeletons finely carved. Easy enough to imagine here the scene of Durdles's drunken sleep, the wicker bottle beside him, on the night when Jasper borrows his keys for some dark purpose.

'The lantern is not wanted, for the moonlight strikes in at the groined windows, bare of glass, the broken frames for which cast patterns on the ground. The heavy pillars which support the roof engender masses of black shade, but between them there are lanes of light. Up and down these lanes they walk, Durdles discoursing of the "old 'uns" he yet counts on disinterring, and slapping a wall, in which he considers "a whole family on 'em" to be stoned and earthed up, just as if he were a familiar friend of the family.'

The Mystery of Edwin Drood has been solved many times since Dickens left the book unfinished; and yet never solved to anyone's complete satisfaction. In the Crypt of Rochester Cathedral some clue may lie unseen as yet by sharp Dickensian eye. But no tomb which might be that of Mrs Sapsea is to be found in the little graveyard, where, Dickens told Georgina Hogarth one day just before his last visit to Rochester, he would like to be buried.

Did his uncanny perception give him any hint, on that visit, of what was to come—not only in the near future, but long after his time? When Mr Miles the verger saw him wandering about the Cathedral, deep in study of it, his inward eye may have caught the faintest gleam of that brass plate which would one day be fixed in the wall below the familiar monument to Richard Watts, the philanthropist, 'with the effigy of worthy Master Richard starting out of it like a ship's figurehead'. The brass plate is inscribed:

CHARLES DICKENS

Born at Portsmouth Seventh of February
1812. Died at Gadshill Place by Rochester
Ninth of June 1870. Buried in Westminster
Abbey.

To connect his memory with the scenes in
which his earliest and his latest years were
passed and with the associations of Rochester
Cathedral and its neighbourhood which
extended over all his life
This tablet with the sanction of the Dean
and Chapter is placed by his Executors.

Before the tablet is the marble tomb and effigy of Dean Hole, who is the Dean of *The Mystery of Edwin Drood*.

Gazing at Eastgate House, from which he had banished Rosa to Staple Inn, he would see, through the mists of time, an inscription calling it 'The Nuns' House of Charles Dickens's *Edwin Drood*', and would see that part of it is a Dickens Museum; while in the garden where Rosa was so terrified by Jasper's proposal, his very own Swiss chalet would look benevolently down upon him. And everywhere, in cafés and antique shops, on shop-fronts, in and about the Bull, would be signs and tokens that this was the Rochester of Charles Dickens, and that he was its proudest possession, though a century had passed since he lived.

He had looked his last on London, a few days before: had, perhaps, taken a stroll to Staple Inn in Holborn, and gazed up at the letters 'P.J.T.' above the door of that legal nook, which so exercised the mind of Mr Grewgious. Even he can hardly have conceived the ruin which would one day fall upon that lovely place from the sky; or that it would be faithfully rebuilt, and P.J.T. restored to his place, in honour of Mr Grewgious and his creator.

On Tuesday, 7th June, he was too tired to go for his usual long walk. Instead, he drove with Georgina to Cobham Woods, dismissed the carriage, and walked round the park and back. That evening he put up some Chinese lanterns, which had arrived during the afternoon, in the new conservatory of which he was so proud; and sat with Georgina in the dining-room all evening, admiring the effect of them when lighted. He had shown the conservatory off to his daughter Katey (now married and living in London) and they had sat there until three o'clock in the morning, talking of things which Katey would never tell anybody in detail. 'He talked and talked—*how* he talked!'

When Katey was about to leave with her sister for town, the following morning, she went to say goodbye to her father, who was working in the chalet. She was half way through the tunnel on her way back to the house when some instinct told her to go back to him. A second, unusually tender, farewell was said.

On Wednesday, 8th June, he worked all morning on *Edwin Drood*, apparently in good spirits, until an hour before his usual dinner time. At dinner Georgina noticed his changed colour and expression. 'For an hour,' he then told her, 'he had been very ill,' but she was to take no notice—dinner must go on. Then he began to talk, rapidly and disconnectedly, of a sale at a neighbour's house, of Macready and Forster, and said that after dinner he would go to London. He rose unsteadily to his feet, and Georgina ran to steady him, begging him to let her help him to lie down. 'Yes,' he replied, 'on the ground,' and fell heavily on his left side.

Those were the last words he spoke. The servants lifted him on to a sofa, hard and scantily upholstered, and wrapped him in a rug. Hot bricks were placed at his feet. Watched by his family—Georgina, both daughters, his son Charley and Ellen—he lay breathing stertorously all night and all next day; until, about six on the evening of 9th June, a tear rolled down his cheek, and, with a shudder and a sigh, he died.

Victorian custom was to rush to the windows the moment a death had occurred, and draw all blinds and curtains. But because Dickens was Dickens, loving fresh air and light so much, they left him lying in the sunlight, looking towards his conservatory and the bright lanterns, with heaps of flowers about him: the blue of lobelia and the brilliant scarlet of his favourites, geraniums, throwing colour up to the high ceiling and reflecting themselves in the pictures and mirrors on the walls.

Only two evenings before, sitting with Georgina in the conservatory, he had told her how happy he was to be at 'Gad's' again; how he wanted his name to be more and more associated with the house and the district, and how he looked forward to lying at last by Rochester Cathedral. Now that he was dead, the family decided at first that little Shorne churchyard, which he had also mentioned, would be a better place, but the Rochester authorities staked a claim for an intra-mural grave for him in the Cathedral, the old burial-ground in the moat having been closed. At the same time the Dean of Westminster was making his own plans to secure another genius for the Abbey; and on 14th June Dickens was laid there, in the quiet, private manner he had wished for, in Poets' Corner, and Dean Stanley said over him the burial service which he had quoted on what was to be almost the last page of *Edwin Drood*, 'preaching the Resurrection and the Life'.

The flat pavement-stone that marks his grave, giving only his name and the dates of his birth and death, looks incongruous among the florid monuments of the Abbey. He would make tart comments on his involuntary companionship with Old Parr, and Charles II's faithful Chiffinch, and that curious hotch-potch of actors and worthies assembled in Poets' Corner. No use to look for him here. If anywhere, one must find him at Gadshill.

It is a brilliant June day, like his last one on earth. Down the road, old Rochester is awake and bustling; the 'queer old clock' on the Town Hall keeps steady time. 'Changes of glorious light' are moving on the trees in his garden, so much taller than when he knew them, the birds sing as cheerfully as when they were wont to fly in and out of his room up among the branches as though it were another nest. But the chalet has gone from its place in the shrubbery, and the bright flower-filled conservatory has gone from the side of the house. From the dining-room comes the chant and chatter of schoolgirl voices, and a sharp call to order and a scampering of young feet.

For a hundred years have passed; standing in the hot June sunshine in his garden at Gadshill, where so much seems unchanged, one is filled with a sudden sense of desolation; for he is not there.

Select Bibliography

ADDISON, WILLIAM, *In the Steps of Charles Dickens*, Rich & Cowan, 1955.

ADRIAN, ARTHUR A., *Georgina Hogarth and the Dickens Circle*, Oxford University Press, 1957.

AYLMER, FELIX, *Dickens Incognito*, Hart-Davis, 1959.

BENTLEY, NICOLAS, *The Victorian Scene: 1837–1901*, Weidenfeld & Nicolson, 1968.

BOYLE, SIR COURTENAY (ed.), *Mary Boyle, Her Book*, John Murray, 1902.

COOPER, T. P., *With Dickens in Yorkshire*, Ben Johnson & Co., 1923.

CRUICKSHANK, R. J., *Charles Dickens and Early Victorian England*, Sir Isaac Pitman & Sons, 1949.

DEXTER, WALTER, *The Kent of Dickens*, Cecil Palmer, 1924.

DOLBY, GEORGE, *Charles Dickens As I Knew Him*, T. Fisher Unwin, 1885.

FITZGERALD, PERCY, *Bozland: Dickens's Places and People*, Downey & Co., 1895. *The Life of Charles Dickens*, Chatto & Windus, 1905.

FLETCHER, GEOFFREY, *London's River*, Hutchinson, 1966.

FORSTER, JOHN, *The Life of Charles Dickens*, Chapman & Hall, 1876. New edition with additional material by A. J. Hoppé, Dent, 1966.

FROST, THOMAS, *In Kent with Charles Dickens*, Tinsley Bros., 1880.

GADD, W. LAWRENCE, '*The Great Expectations' Country*, Cecil Palmer, 1929.

HIBBERT, CHRISTOPHER, *The Making of Charles Dickens*, Longmans, 1967.

KENT, WILLIAM, *London for Dickens Lovers*, Methuen, 1935.

KITTON, F. G., *The Dickens Country*, Adam & Charles Black, 1905.

LANGTON, ROBERT, *The Childhood and Youth of Charles Dickens*, Hutchinson, revised edition, 1912.

MATZ, B. W., *Dickensian Inns and Taverns*, Cecil Palmer, 1922.

PRIESTLEY, J. B., *Charles Dickens: A Pictorial Biography*, Thames & Hudson, 1961.

WARD, H. SNOWDEN *and* CATHERINE WEED BARNES, *The Real Dickens Land*, Chapman and Hall, 1904.

The Dickensian, published annually by the Dickens Fellowship.

Index

Italic numerals refer to plates

Bow (E. London), 4, 75
Bowes, Yorkshire, 69–71, *14*
Bradbury and Evans (publishers), 121
Brain, W. Russell, 13on.
Bridgenorth, Shropshire, 85
'Brig Place', 96
Brighton, 3, 96–7, 98, 138, *16*: Old Ship, 96
Bristol: Bush, 60
Broadstairs, Kent, 3, 76–80, 83, 86, 118, 125, 139, *36*; Dickens House, 79, *18*; Fort House, 3, 77, 78, 123, *17*; Tartar Frigate, 79
Brompton, 49–50, 73
Browne, Hablot K. (illustrator); *see* 'Phiz'
Bulwer-Lytton, Sir Edward, 112–114, *28*
Bury St Edmunds, Suffolk, 57, 138, 154: Angel, 58; Southgate House, 58
Bushey, Hertfordshire, 84
Byron, George Gordon, Lord, 21, 125

Camden Town, 19–21, 22, 31, 93, 98, 127: Mother Redcap (public house), 20
Canterbury, 101–3, 104, 120, 138, 152: Fountain Hotel, 102, 152; Sun, 102, 103
Canvey Island, 137
Carlisle, 138, 139
Carlyle, Jane, 1, 63
Carlyle, Thomas, 138
Cattermole, George (illustrator), 84, 85–6, 88, 89, 113, *19*
Chalk, Kent, 52–3, 54, 131, *31*: churchyard, 132
Chalk Farm, 20
Chapman and Hall (publishers), 51, 142n.
'Charitable Grinders' school', 98
Charles Dickens Primary School, 25
Chatham, Kent, 6, 11–18, 21, 49,
101, 111, 125, 127, 132, *3*: dockyard, 12, 16–17; Mitre, 15, 156; St Mary's Church, 16
Cheadle, Cheshire: George and Dragon, 116
Cheltenham, 138
Chertsey, Surrey, 143: Pycroft House, 4, 67
'Chesney Wold', 107–8, *26*
Chester, 138, 149
Chigwell, Essex: King's Head, 5, 87–90, *21*
Churches, *see under* London and individual towns
'Clennam, Mrs', house of, 5, *2*
Cliffe, Kent, 131, 132
'Cloisterham', 154, 155
Coaching days, 45–8
'Coavinses' Castle', 109
Cobham, Kent, 54, 124, 151, 159: Leather Bottle, 53–4, 81n., 151–152, *37*
'Coketown', 115–17
Colchester, Essex, 138
Collins, Wilkie, 139
Collins' Farm, Hampstead, 63–4, 65, *13*
'Commodore' (stage-coach), 56
'Cook's Court', 109
Cooling, Kent, 152: churchyard, 128–30, *32*
Cornwall, 138
Coventry, 84
Cowper, William, 94
Cruikshank, George (illustrator), 32, 78
'Crupps's, Mrs', 103

Danson, Dr Henry, 33
Dartford, Kent, 120
Davis, Mrs (landlady), 41
Deal, Kent, 111–12: Royal (Three Kings) Hotel, 111
'Dedlock Arms', 108
Dent, J. M., and Sons Ltd (publishers), 30
Dickens, Alfred (brother), 19